SECRET

STRASBOURG

Guillaume Bouvier, Véronique Herbreteau and Isabelle Kapp

JONGLEZ PUBLISHING

Travel guides

Guillaume Bouvier has a PhD in History and Ancient Sciences. After a career as a palaeographer and archaeologist, his passion for writing led him to become an author, translator and editorial manager. He has lived in Strasbourg since 1990.

Véronique Herbreteau holds a bachelor's degree in Art History and a master's degree in Museology. Born in Strasbourg to an Alsatian family, she has been a tour guide and lecturer for over 20 years. She offers her clients classic or unusual tours in Strasbourg and elsewhere in Alsace, which have earned her the distinction of being the region's first medal-winning tour guide.

Isabelle Kapp has a PhD in art history and is a clinical psychologist. She has taught in France and abroad, notably at the University of Szczecin (Poland) and Centre College in Strasbourg. A specialist in Art Nouveau and passionate about Strasbourg's heritage, she is also an independent tour guide and lecturer, offering tours, conferences and publications that bring together the city's history, art and memory.

We have taken great pleasure in drawing up 'Secret Strasbourg' and hope that through its guidance you will, like us, continue to discover unusual, hidden or little-known aspects of the city. Descriptions of certain places are accompanied by thematic sections highlighting historical details or anecdotes as an aid to understanding the city in all its complexity.
'Secret Strasbourg' also draws attention to the multitude of details found in places that we may pass every day without noticing.
These are an invitation to look more closely at the urban landscape and, more generally, a means of seeing our own city with the curiosity and attention that we often display while travelling elsewhere ...

Comments on this guide and its contents, as well as information on sites not mentioned, are welcome and will help us to enrich future editions.

Don't hesitate to contact us:
E-mail: info@jonglezpublishing.com

N
BRUMATH, HAGUENAU
D185
D263
Bischheim
D468
A35
D120
D120
Schiltigheim
D263
D468
Aar
D31
A350
Cronenbourg
Place de Haguenau
D41
Neustadt
SAVERNE
Place de la République
A35
A351
p. 12
Gare Centrale
STRASBOURG
Place Kléber
Petite France
Ill
Koenigshoffen
N4
D392
Montagne Verte
A352
N83
Bruche
D392
Elsau
A35
Ill
Murhof
Niederwald
Canal du Rhône au Rhin
Aéroport de Strasbourg-Entzheim
Étang Gerig
Meinau
N83
p. 264
SÉLESTAT, COLMAR

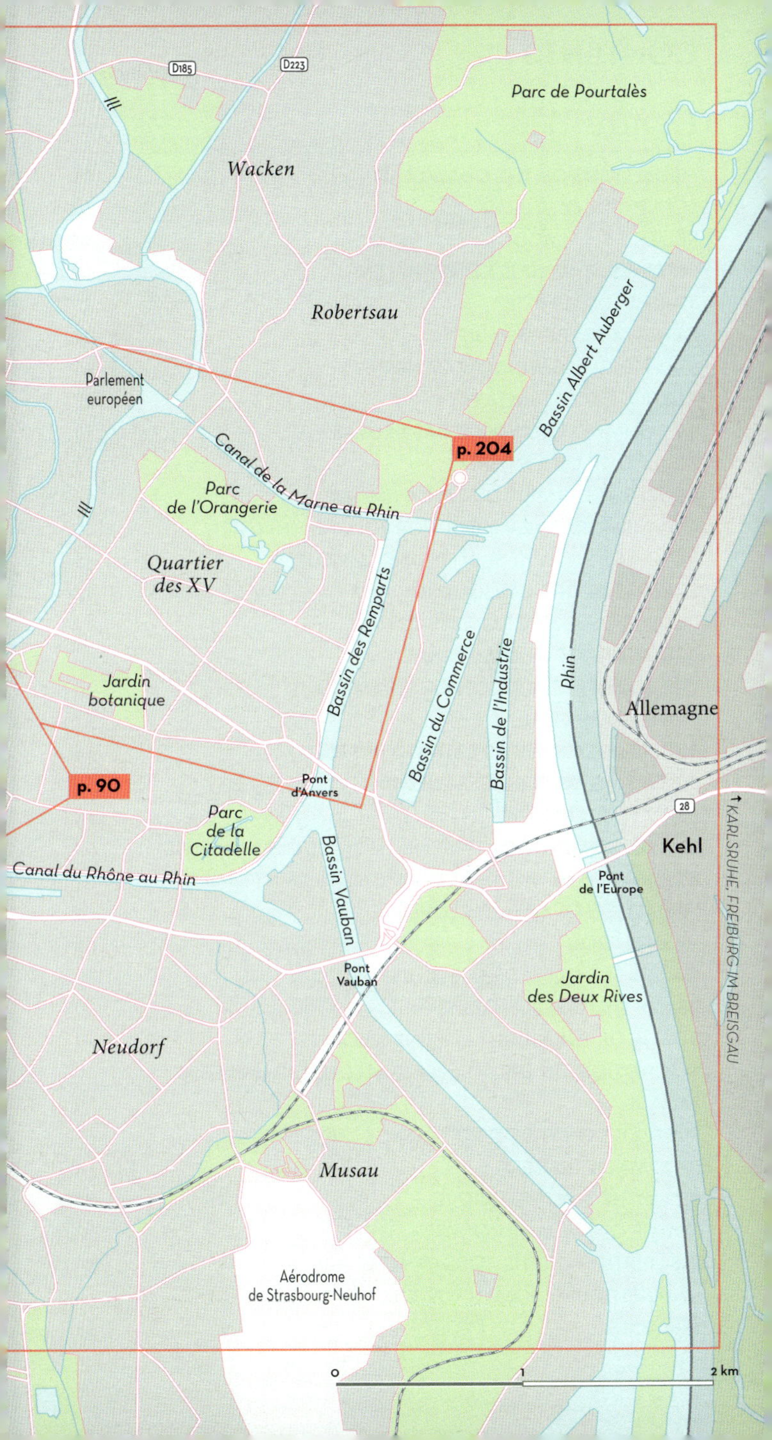

D185
D223
Parc de Pourtalès
Wacken
Robertsau
Parlement européen
Bassin Albert Auberger
p. 204
Canal de la Marne au Rhin
Parc de l'Orangerie
Quartier des XV
Bassin des Remparts
Bassin du Commerce
Bassin de l'Industrie
Rhin
Allemagne
Jardin botanique
p. 90
Pont d'Anvers
Parc de la Citadelle
Canal du Rhône au Rhin
Bassin Vauban
28
Kehl
Pont de l'Europe
KARLSRUHE, FREIBURG-IM-BREISGAU
Pont Vauban
Jardin des Deux Rives
Neudorf
Musau
Aérodrome de Strasbourg-Neuhof
0
1
2 km

CONTENTS

Centre West

Centre East

CONTENTS

Neustadt

Outside the centre

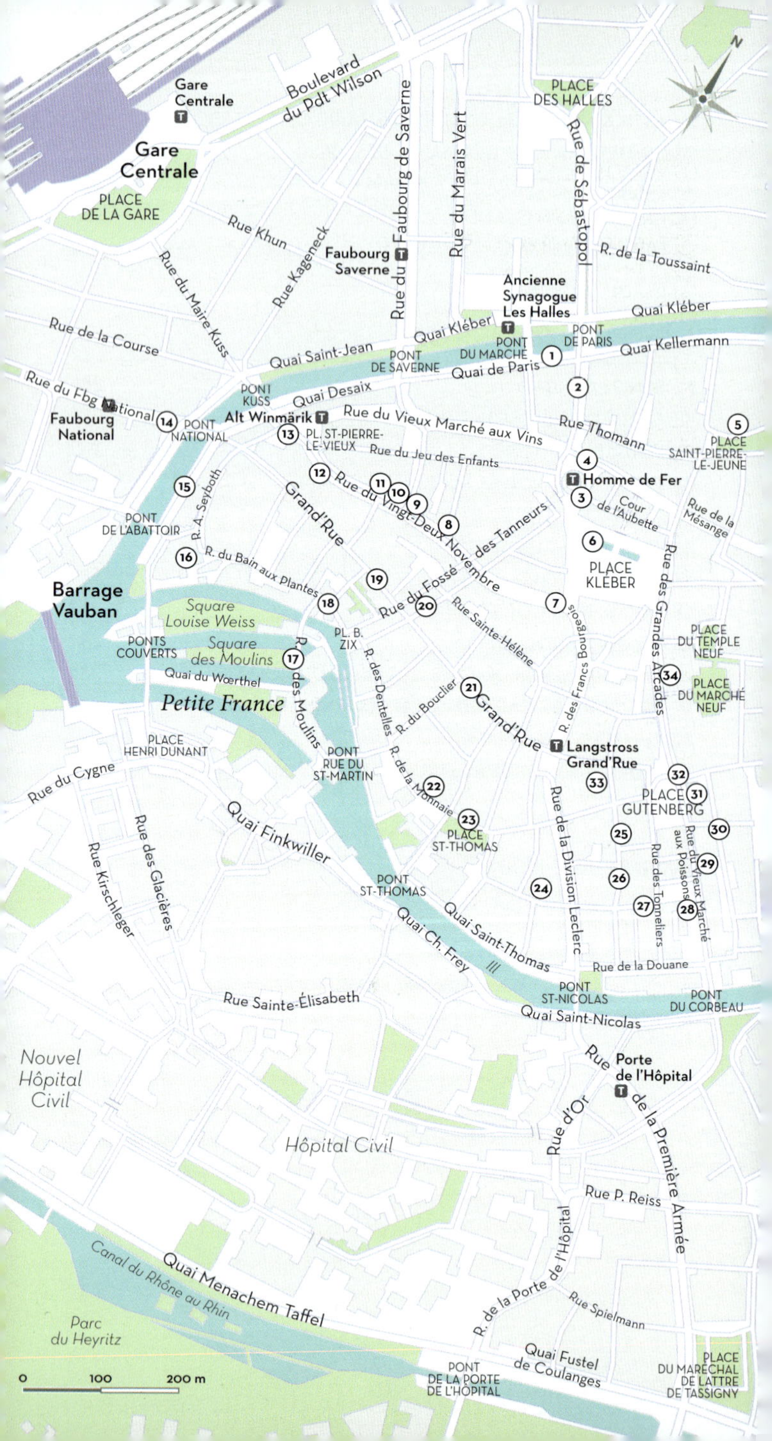

Gare Centrale
Gare Centrale
PLACE DE LA GARE
Boulevard du Pdt Wilson
Rue du Faubourg de Saverne
Rue du Marais Vert
PLACE DES HALLES
Rue de Sébastopol
Rue Khun
Rue Kageneck
Faubourg Saverne
R. de la Toussaint
Ancienne Synagogue Les Halles
Quai Kléber
Rue du Maire Kuss
Rue de la Course
Quai Saint-Jean
Quai Kléber
PONT DE PARIS
PONT DU MARCHÉ
PONT DE SAVERNE
Quai de Paris
Quai Kellermann
Rue du Fbg National
Faubourg National
PONT KUSS
Quai Desaix
Alt Winmärik
PONT NATIONAL
PL. ST-PIERRE-LE-VIEUX
Rue du Vieux Marché aux Vins
Rue Thomann
PLACE SAINT-PIERRE-LE-JEUNE
Rue du Jeu des Enfants
Homme de Fer
R. A. Seyboth
Rue du Vingt-Deux Novembre
Grand'Rue
Cour de l'Aubette
Rue de la Mésange
PONT DE L'ABATTOIR
des Tanneurs
R. du Bain aux Plantes
Rue du Fossé
PLACE KLÉBER
Barrage Vauban
Square Louise Weiss
Rue Sainte-Hélène
R. des Francs Bourgeois
Rue des Grandes Arcades
PONTS COUVERTS
Square des Moulins
PL. B. ZIX
PLACE DU TEMPLE NEUF
Quai du Wœrthel
R. des Moulins
R. des Dentelles
R. du Bouclier
PLACE DU MARCHÉ NEUF
Petite France
Grand'Rue
Langstross Grand'Rue
PLACE HENRI DUNANT
PONT RUE DU ST-MARTIN
R. de la Monnaie
PLACE GUTENBERG
Rue du Cygne
Rue de la Division Leclerc
Rue des Glacières
Quai Finkwiller
PLACE ST-THOMAS
Rue du Vieux Marché aux Poissons
Rue Kirschleger
PONT ST-THOMAS
Rue des Tonneliers
Quai Ch. Frey
Quai Saint-Thomas
Ill
Rue de la Douane
Rue Sainte-Élisabeth
PONT ST-NICOLAS
PONT DU CORBEAU
Quai Saint-Nicolas
Nouvel Hôpital Civil
Porte de l'Hôpital
Rue de la Première Armée
Hôpital Civil
Rue d'Or
Rue P. Reiss
R. de la Porte de l'Hôpital
Quai Menachem Taffel
Canal du Rhône au Rhin
Rue Spielmann
Parc du Heyritz
Quai Fustel de Coulanges
PONT DE LA PORTE DE L'HÔPITAL
PLACE DU MARÉCHAL DE LATTRE DE TASSIGNY
0
100
200 m

Centre West

MEDALLIONS ON THE QUAI KLÉBER

1

The memory of a lost station

Wall below the Quai Kléber, alongside the Canal des Faux Remparts, between the Pont de Paris and the Pont du Marché

Below the Quai Kléber, on the banks of the Ill, a series of 11 medallions can be seen embedded in the wall of the quay. From left to right, they feature the coats of arms of Paris, Châlons, Bar-le-Duc, Metz, Nancy, Alsace-Lorraine, Wissembourg, Strasbourg, Colmar, Mulhouse and Basel.

These sculpted medallions are the last surviving vestiges of Strasbourg's former railway station, demolished in 1974 (despite public protest) to make way for the shopping centre on the Place des Halles.

Originally displayed on the façade of the old passenger building, they were preserved and repositioned a few metres from their initial location. They serve as a reminder of the railway lines that once connected to Strasbourg.

The old Strasbourg station, sometimes known as the Marais-Vert station, was inaugurated in 1846 and stood close to the city's historic centre. It closed to passengers in 1883 following the opening of the current main station, Strasbourg-Ville.

Afterwards, the former passenger building was repurposed as a covered market, and the bridge in front, once called Pont de la Gare, was renamed Pont du Marché – a name it still bears today.

The station's buffet remained open on its original premises for many years, providing a convenient location for resistance fighters to exchange messages between 1940 and 1944. The railway tracks were left intact and continued to carry freight trains, including those supplying the market.

From the 1950s onwards, the site also hosted a bus station and a flea market, held along Rue de Sébastopol.

The small street linking Rue du Marais Vert to Rue des Halles was named Rue de l'Ancienne Gare in memory of the lost station.

The small street connecting Rue du Marais Vert to Rue des Halles was named 'Rue de l'Ancienne Gare' in memory of this lost monument.

SCULPTURE OF A BEAR

②

A bear in the city

5, rue du Noyer
Tram A, D – Homme de Fer stops

Since 2015, a monumental bear sculpture has stood watch over 5 Rue du Noyer from a recess on the third floor of the building's façade, just above the shop.

Created by artists Antoine Immersion and Christophe Wehrung, both former students of HEAR (Haute École des Arts du Rhin), this remarkable work remains surprisingly little known despite its imposing 5-metre height.

Contrary to some claims, the sculpture was not intended as a tribute to the history of the street, which in the 18th century was known as 'Ruelle de l'Ours' (Bear Street).

The artists were simply commissioned by the architects of the 'Le Plaza' real estate project, who wanted to incorporate a sculpture into the building. Among the early proposals, the bear was chosen and retained.

RELIEF OF A PEACOCK

③

Allusion to a former owner

2, place de l'Homme-de-Fer
Tram A, D – Homme de Fer stop

Built in 1768 for Philippe Jacques Faudel, the building at No. 2 Place de l'Homme de Fer is a fine example of Strasbourg's Rococo architecture.

Alongside the famous 'Iron Man' decorating the façade, a discreet but meaningful detail deserves attention: the relief of a peacock on the arch of the central entrance.

Carved with great finesse – each feather precisely rendered – the peacock alludes to the name of the building's former owner. Faudel echoes the German word *Pfauel* (derived from *Pfau*, 'peacock'), playfully hinting at 'little peacock'.

On either side of the bird, faces above the windows represent the four seasons: on the left, a grotesque figure with flowers for spring and one with ears of wheat for summer; on the right, a bunch of grapes for autumn and a bearded old man for winter.

Higher up, a woodland fauna decorates the first-floor window, which is surmounted by the figure of Mercury on the second floor. Around them appear the four continents: helmeted Europe, Asia with a turban, Africa with an elephant's trunk, and America.

LATRINES AT No. 9, RUE SAINTE-HÉLÈNE

④

In Renaissance times, it was best to avoid walking near the walls...

9, rue Sainte-Hélène

Built on the site of a former beguinage, the beautiful Renaissance house at 9, rue Sainte-Hélène stands out for its preserved arcaded galleries (dating to 1632) and vividly restored frescoes (restored in 1991).

Listed as a Historic Monument since 1984, the U-shaped building features a peaceful inner courtyard accessible from the street.

But one lesser-known feature hides at the back : a surviving set of projecting latrines – believed to be Strasbourg's last remaining examples.

Miraculously spared during the creation of Rue du 22 Novembre, they extend over a preserved section of alleyway.

To understand the function (and pollution) of these waste-disposal facilities, the *Allmendbuch* (Commons Register) of 1587 distinguishes three types of latrines (known as *Profeÿ*).

The first, built outside and fenced off, could be shared daily by several dozen residents.

The other two types were attached to the wall over the street and used either closed or open waste systems.

The open type, known as *Sprôchhîser* ('chatrooms'), were supposed to be located on either side of the *Fossé des Tanneurs* (Tanners' Ditch). As no pipes were planned, they emptied straight into this open-air cesspool that ran through the city from west to east, carrying waste from the tanneries (see following double-page spread).

However, a look at the base of latrines on Rue Sainte-Hélène shows that the right side was sealed off some time after the houses were built. Given the street's proximity to Tanners' Ditch, this waste-disposal method also seems to have been authorised.

In the 17th century it was wise to avoid walking too close to buildings, as all kinds of filth could be thrown to the ground for collection.

But the garbage collector rarely passed, so best stick to the middle of the street ...

Strasbourg in the Middle Ages : streets littered with rubbish

For an authentic view of Strasbourg's sanitary conditions from the Middle Ages to the early 20th century, note that human and animal waste was everywhere.

A 1628 police decree allowed each household to raise two pigs and 24 geese.

Despite endless official warnings, the Strasbourgeois were reluctant to clear up animal droppings ...

Legally they had to dump manure at four designated sites, including the horse market in what is now Place Broglie, but compliance was low.

In 1635 the roads were said to be so dirty and littered with rubbish that the city debated hiring workers from the nearby villages to clean them.

These clean-ups were so rare that in 1620 someone took the trouble to record that Place Saint-Martin (now Place Gutenberg) had just been swept ...

Apart from animal waste, citizens were supposed to clean the street opposite their home and take their own rubbish out of the city. Few did so ...

The very irregular passage of the Horblohner (garbage trucks) was nowhere near enough, so the streets of Strasbourg were generally full of filth.

As most streets were paved in a 'V' shape, in heavy rain the central drainage channel quickly turned into an open-air sewer, often blocked and emitting all kinds of foul smells.

It's true that the city sometimes hired a 'mud master' to shovel out this sludge.

But only in the early 18th century did Strasbourg finally begin to pave its streets like a roadway, with a curved profile and a drain on each side some distance from the rows of houses.

The 'Fossé des Tanneurs' : a former open sewer

Tanners' Ditch, an insanitary canal like the Bièvre in Paris, has run through Strasbourg from west to east since the Middle Ages at least.

This open sewer carried human waste from riverside houses and runoff from the tanneries.

In 1954, a survey found that 93% of homes lacked toilet facilities in the run-down and dilapidated neighbourhood of Petite France, and 7% had no running water.

A Housing Inspection Commission set up in 1898 (when Strasbourg was a German city) deplored the outdated city-centre housing.

Investigations highlighted residents' misery in squalid living conditions that had barely attracted official attention.

High rates of tuberculosis and infant mortality reflected a general lack of hygiene, while limited access to latrines contributed to the spread of infectious diseases.

As did the lack of sunlight, ventilation and heating, and in this dense urban framework two-thirds of the city streets were less than 3 metres wide.

Major redevelopment work to upgrade the road network and surroundings began in 1907, when 126 houses were demolished in order to make way for new housing, shops and general urban renewal.

This project, known as the 'Grande Percée' ('Great Breakthrough'), was intended to link the station to Place de la Bourse via a new street, now Rue du 22 Novembre.

The excavation work created another issue: it also meant moving the evicted families.

Several housing estates on the outskirts (including Stockfeld garden city) were built to relocate people from the old city centre. The last of these was only completed in the 1960s.

Rue du Fossé des Tanneurs is the result of filling in the canal – work started between 1840 and 1842 was not completed until after 1876.

'CHEMIN DE LUMIÈRE'

⑤

A spiritual and initiatory journey for believers

Église protestante Saint-Pierre-le-Jeune
Place Saint-Pierre-le-Jeune
Daily 12pm–6pm
Tram A, D – Homme de Fer stop
Tram C – Place Broglie stop

Also known as the 'Sentier de la Vertu' (Path of Virtue) or the 'Chemin du Ciel' (Way of Heaven), the 'Chemin de Lumière' (Way of Light) is a discreet mystical route built into the choir floor of the Protestant church of Saint-Pierre-le-Jeune.

This path, traced by lines of lead embedded in the stone, guides the faithful from the entrance of the choir to the altar.

Through this symbolic journey, the believer treads on various representations of creatures – the dragon (symbol of evil and chaos), the lion (representing violence and pride), and vipers (symbols of cunning and sin) – each evoking a temptation or trial that a Christian must face and overcome.

The path forms a Latin cross, and the use of lead – a heavy, durable material – evokes the perseverance required in faith.

After crossing this obstacle-laden path, the faithful reach the altar, representing the heavenly Jerusalem – the divine city promised to believers. The path then extends around the altar, revealing the four rivers of Paradise mentioned in the Book of Genesis, symbols of eternal life and divine grace.

The Way of Light embodies the journey of the Christian soul: an initiatory path from confrontation with evil to union with God. Each step represents a spiritual victory over the forces of evil, marking a progression of inner purification.

Psalm 91:13 illustrates this perfectly: 'You will tread on the lion and the cobra; you will trample the great lion and the serpent.'

By trampling these creatures, the believer symbolically triumphs over temptation, progressing towards holiness.

The ultimate reward for this journey is the crown of life (depicted at the foot of the choir, near the altar from which the rivers of Paradise flow), promised to those who have persevered.

Having overcome earthly temptations, the faithful are welcomed into the divine presence – a symbol of eternal communion with God.

GENERAL KLÉBER'S VAULT

⑥

Kléber's tomb in a public car park

Place Kléber
Parking Kléber - Homme de Fer

General Jean-Baptiste Kléber (1753–1800), hero of the French Revolution who distinguished himself during the War in the Vendée and the Egyptian Campaign, is remembered today by a well-known bronze statue in the square that bears his name.

Yet few realise that this monument sits above the vault in which Kléber's ashes were deposited, and that his tomb is now located in an underground car park.

The trials and tribulations of the general's remains know no bounds.

In the first place, after he was assassinated by a young Egyptian Muslim in the gardens of his Cairo residence, 14 June 1800, back in France the question of how to suitably commemorate his status and qualities prompted heated debate.

After many aberrations his remains were transported to his hometown Strasbourg in 1818.

It was planned to bury them in Notre-Dame cathedral, where a vault had been prepared in Saint-Laurent chapel.

His remains were moved again on 13 December 1838 to Place d'Armes (now Place Kléber).

The statue by Philippe Grass (1801–76), was unveiled on 14 June 1840, 40 years to the day after the general's death. At the same time the square was renamed in his honour.

But the adventures of Kléber's ashes didn't stop there: during the German Occupation they were transferred to the military cemetery of Cronenbourg, below a simple wooden cross, and his statue was also removed and the square renamed (see below).

After the Liberation, the general's remains were again moved, back to the vault in Place Kléber, and his statue reinstated.

Yet another twist occurred in 1967, when the city planned an underground car park in the square. Rather than move the tomb again, planners chose to bypass it ...

A commemorative plaque now marks the site of Kléber's remains, which lie on the other side of a wall in the parking space.

Place Kléber renamed under the Occupation

During World War II, Place Kléber was renamed Karl-Roos-Platz, after Karl-Philipp Roos (1878–1940), an Alsatian Nazi sympathiser and German spy.

He was executed by the French on 7 February 1940 in Champigneulles, near Nancy, and was later venerated by the Nazi regime.

STAINED-GLASS WINDOW OF HERMES

⑦

A Greek divinity at the service of 20th-century trade

Galeries Lafayette, corner of Rue du 22 Novembre and Rue des Francs-Bourgeois
Free guided tours (French) : Wednesday & Friday, 10am–11am (groups of 5–10)
Booking required : 03 88 16 57 12 or by email to: accueil.info@galerieslafayette.com

Hidden away on the fourth floor of Galeries Lafayette is a stunning coloured-glass panel, little known even among Strasbourg locals. Created in 1914 and restored for the centenary of the 'Grand Magasin' (see below), the window is reached by a beautifully crafted oak staircase decorated with floral balustrades, stuccoed mouldings and ornate handrails.

The stained glass depicts Hermes, the Greek god of commerce (Mercury to the Romans), surrounded by flowers and fruits symbolising abundance and prosperity.

Strategically installed in the highest part of the building to watch over the store (and especially the customers), this symbol embodies the commercial spirit of the place.

Outside, the building's prosperity is echoed in the sculpted caryatids facing Rue du 22 Novembre. Created by Charles-Albert Schultz, these four female figures represent the seasons, reinforcing the store's success across the year.

The 'Grand Magasin' in Strasbourg

Strasbourg's Grand Magasin was constructed between 1911 and 1912, during the city's ambitious urban renewal effort known as the 'Great Breakthrough' (see p. 21). Designed by architects Jules Berninger and Henri-Gustave Krafft, it opened in 1914 as the Kaufhaus Modern.

Shortly thereafter, it was requisitioned during World War I and used as a flour depot. Post-war, the name was changed to Magasins Modernes in 1919, and abbreviated to Magmod in 1924.

In 1940, under Nazi occupation, it was handed to the Union company, and by 1945 it reverted to Magmod. It later became Nouvelles Galeries in 1982 and finally Galeries Lafayette in 2000. Today, with 12,500 square metres of retail space, this is the largest Galeries Lafayette location outside Paris.

VESTIGE OF A FOUNTAIN

8

Memory of an ancient activity relating to water

4, rue des Aveugles
Tram A, D – Homme de Fer stop

In the heart of the historic centre, at 4, rue des Aveugles, one might easily overlook a grey object set at chest height between two windows on the first floor of a red-brick building.

It consists of a carved cast-iron column and a small tap pointing into empty space: the upper part of an old fountain, reused as an ornament when the building was constructed in 1912.

Beneath the column, an elegantly curved rod supports two wrought-iron letters 'F' that bear its weight.

For more than a century, the building was associated with water-related trades. In 1912 it became home to the Ch. & E. Möbs company, specialists in sanitary installations.

Several members of the Möbs family both lived and worked there. The tradition continued until 2018 with Hydro Industrie, another company in the same sector.

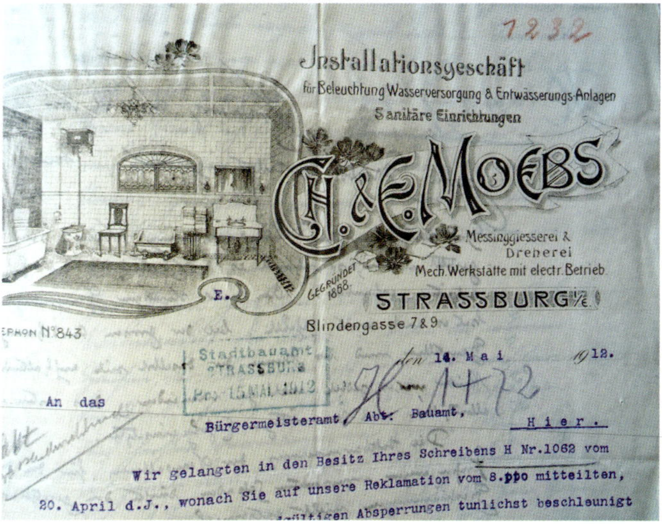

Jnstallationsgeschäft
für Beleuchtung Wasserversorgung & Entwässerungs-Anlagen
Sanitäre Einrichtungen
Ch. & E. Moebs
Messinggiesserei & Dreherei
Mech. Werkstätte mit electr. Betrieb
Gegründet 1868
STRASSBURG i/E.
Blindengasse 7 & 9
...phon No 843

Stadtbauamt Strassburg 15 MAI 1912

den 14. Mai 1912.

An das Bürgermeisteramt, Abt. Bauamt, Hier.

Wir gelangten in den Besitz Ihres Schreibens H Nr.1062 vom 20. April d.J., wonach Sie auf unsere Reklamation vom 8.pbo mitteilten, ... Absperrungen tunlichst beschleunigt

'LE SON' AND 'LA LUMIÈRE' BAS-RELIEFS ⑨

Copy of bas-reliefs from New York Rockefeller Center

16, rue du 22 Novembre
Tram A, D – Homme de Fer stop – Grand'Rue stop

On the façade of an otherwise unassuming building at 16, rue du 22 Novembre, two striking bas-reliefs catch the eye.

'Le Son' (Sound) is represented by a naked man, crouching as if emerging from the celestial vault, with one hand cupped to his mouth to amplify a cry that seems to escape in concentric circles, reminiscent of sound waves. His other hand is placed near his ear, as if perceiving invisible vibrations. The 'Le Son' bas-relief almost suggests a biblical scene – the first human producing the first sound, the very source of the creation of the world.

The bas-relief to the right, 'La Lumière' (Light), depicts a naked woman with flowing, serrated hair, moving among the clouds. Facing a stylised light source – a symbol of progress and modernity emerging from the clouds – she forms a counterpart to the male figure.

'Le Son' and 'La Lumière' are both carved in a pure Art Deco style (artist unknown), set above the windows of a former shop once named Tiffany, after the famous New York jeweller on Fifth Avenue.

These works are copies of originals made in 1935 by American sculptor Lee Lawrie for the Rockefeller Center in New York. Old photographs show no trace of these copies before 1942.

Could this be an allegory of the creation of the world through an Art Deco version of Adam and Eve? It would not be surprising.

The bas-relief entitled 'Wisdom', above the main entrance to the Rockefeller Center and flanked by 'Sound' on the left and 'Light' on the right, is itself inspired by a biblical passage (Isaiah 33:6), which states: 'Wisdom and knowledge shall be the stability of thy times.'

The depiction of 'Wisdom', a bearded old man dissipating the clouds of ignorance and bearing a striking resemblance to God, is directly inspired by William Blake's vision of Jehovah.

© PortableNYCTours

SCULPTURE OF A MINER ⑩

A tribute to industrial trades

16, rue du 22 Novembre
Tram A, D – Homme de Fer stop

Discreetly placed on the façade of 16, rue du 22 Novembre, a bas-relief carved in the 1920s or 1930s depicts a helmeted miner, kneeling with his lantern and staff.

This sculpture was part of a symbolic decorative programme common in Art Nouveau and Art Deco architecture (late 19th / early 20th century), particularly in industrial or commercial cities such as Strasbourg. At that time, it was customary to decorate buildings with

allegories of trades, especially those that contributed to the wealth or strength of the nation. The miner represents hard work, physical strength and industrial progress.

Between 1871 and 1918, Strasbourg was part of the German Empire. Germany, then a booming industrial power, promoted occupations linked to natural resources such as mining. This sculpture symbolises the industrial modernity pursued by the local authorities along the *Grande Percée* (Great Breakthrough), the modern urban axis then under construction.

The bas-relief refers to the rich seams of potash discovered in Alsace in the early 20th century, a resource that transformed the region's economy and social fabric. These mines, located mainly in the centre of the Haut-Rhin département and to the north of Mulhouse, were gradually shut down from the late 1950s, with permanent closure in 2004.

Beyond this tribute, the sculpture belongs to an artistic tradition where the worker becomes a hero. The miner's squatting posture is far from submissive: on the contrary, it evokes stability and resilience – essential qualities of mining work.

The lantern, central to the composition, symbolises more than its practical purpose. It represents light in darkness, knowledge and vigilance, reminding us that these men, through patience and perseverance, were the guardians of the wealth hidden beneath the ground.

The curved staff, often associated with exploration and caution, reinforces this idea of mastery and protection. Finally, the bird on the cage refers to the canaries once used in mines to detect toxic gases, particularly carbon monoxide.

What is potash?

Potash, derived from the German word *Pottasche* ('ash pot'), is a saline mineral mainly used in the fertiliser industry. Potash salt, commonly known as potash, was once produced by macerating plant ash. Most housewives in the 18th century used this process unknowingly, adding fat to the ash to create washing powder. Today, the main producers of potash are Canada, Russia, Belarus, China and Germany. Around 95% of the potash used in US agriculture is imported, 90% of it from Canada.

RELIEFS AT 12-14, RUE DU 22 NOVEMBRE

11

Masonic-inspired façade

12 and 14, rue du 22 Novembre
Trams A, D – Homme de Fer stops

At the junction of Rue du 22 Novembre and Rue des Aveugles stands a vast building (Nos. 4–14, rue du 22 Novembre), constructed around 1913 by Heinrich Backes and Otto Zache, as recorded by an inscription at the corner.

The five windows on the third floor of Nos. 12–14 are adorned with animal motifs: an owl with a book (symbol of wisdom), two birds (symbols of partnership and love), a rooster (Christian symbol of the triumph of light over darkness), and a dog (symbol of fidelity).

Through these reliefs the architects conveyed moral values such as wisdom, vigilance, freedom, and loyalty, following an artistic tradition in which animals are used to express symbolic and moral messages.

The entrances to the two buildings also feature distinctive sculptures with Masonic inspiration.

The doorway of No. 12 is decorated with a cartouche bearing hammers and children holding tools—possibly an allusion to the Apprentice Mason, at the first stage of evolution, beginning his work on himself.

Above the doorway of No. 14 is a set square and compass, familiar Masonic symbols, accompanied by three small escutcheons. The square, often associated with matter, signifies moral rectitude and 'rectitude in action', while the compass symbolises spirit and denotes 'measure in research'. Intertwined, the two represent the second Masonic grade, that of Companion (see following double-page spread).

Higher up is a depiction of an ancient temple, reminiscent of Solomon's Temple, with a triangular pediment and six columns framed by horns of plenty.

The apprentice of No. 12 has advanced: guided by the moral values represented by the animals in the third-floor windows, he progresses to No. 14 with the rank of Companion, enabling him to move towards the temple of Jerusalem, symbol of the divine presence on Earth.

Although there is no documentary evidence that the building ever housed a Masonic lodge, the whole façade can be read as an allegory of Masonic initiation towards divine light.

Freemason symbolism of square and compass

The square, used to check the angles of a construction, also conveys the lesson 'to act with rectitude, in accordance with the Masonic rule, and to harmonise one's conduct with the principles of morality and virtue'.

A symbol of the Freemason who works on himself to progress from rough stone to cut stone, the square is often associated with matter and signifies 'rectitude in action'.

The compass, with its variable gauge, symbolises the spirit and represents 'measure in research'.

An attentive observer will note that, although the square and compass are often shown together, they are not always represented in the same way – which, of course, has meaning.

When the square is placed above the compass, it refers to the first grade: Apprentice. At this stage, the material (square) still takes precedence over the spirit (compass).

When the two are intertwined, they represent the second degree of Freemasonry: Companion, a stage of evolution where matter and spirit are in balance, a necessary condition for spiritual enlightenment.

Finally, when the compass is shown above the square, it symbolises spirit (spirituality) prevailing over matter (the profane), an initiatory progression marked in the Masonic hierarchy by the third grade: Master Mason.

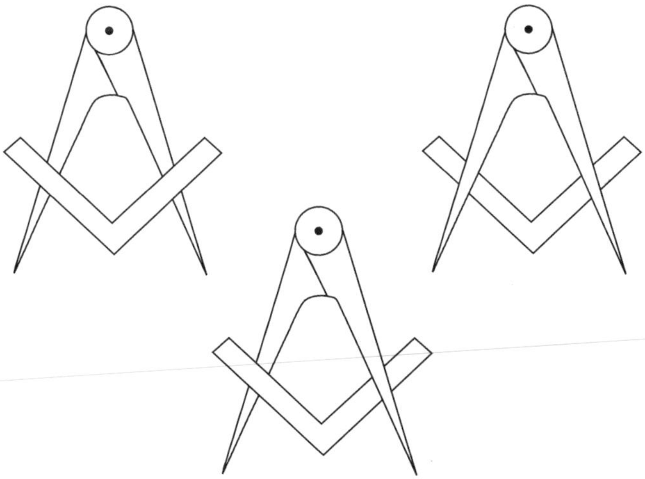

COMMEMORATIVE PLAQUE FOR JOHANN KNAUTH

12

A late tribute to the 'saviour of the Cathedral'

Place de la Cathédrale, near the Post Office entrance
Société des Amis de la Cathédrale de Strasbourg
6, rue du 22 Novembre
03 88 23 28 07
amis-cathedrale-strasbourg.eu

On 27 June 2015, a commemorative plaque was unveiled on Place de la Cathédrale, beside the entrance to the Post Office. Its inscription reads: 'The City of Strasbourg is grateful to Johann Knauth, the saviour of the cathedral. 2014.'

Despite having a street in Strasbourg named after him since 1974, the German architect Johann Knauth (1864–1924) remains largely unknown.

From 1905 to 1920, he was chief architect of the Fondation de l'Œuvre Notre-Dame and of Strasbourg Cathedral.

In 1903, Knauth discovered that work to channel the Rhine had led to a dramatic drop in the water table.

This posed a serious threat to the cathedral's foundations, which rested on oak piles. Submerged wood can remain stable for centuries, but once exposed to air, it begins to rot.

According to Knauth's calculations, the cathedral would eventually collapse if nothing was done.

The pillar of the north tower – built between 1240 and 1270 – was especially vulnerable. Though it bore the entire weight of the 7,500-tonne tower, it had not been designed for such a load. Cracks had appeared in the foundation walls, and the tower was visibly leaning.

Knauth's warnings were finally heeded in 1911. Restoration work, financed in part by Kaiser Wilhelm II, began in 1912. The project involved encasing the large pillar in reinforced concrete and resting it on a new concrete foundation.

The work was still ongoing in 1920 when Knauth, who refused to take French nationality following the end of the war, was dismissed and expelled. His deputy, architect Charles Pierre (1875–1962), completed the restoration in 1926.

At the final ceremony marking the end of the works, Knauth's name was not even mentioned.

At the foot of the now-stabilised pillar stands a small 20-centimetre sculpture nicknamed 'the strong man of the cathedral.' The figure appears to bear the enormous weight of the structure alone. Is it a self-portrait by Charles Pierre – or a discreet tribute to Knauth?

VERONICA'S VEIL AT SAINT-PIERRE-LE-VIEUX

(13)

A little-known episode from the Passion of Jesus

Église Saint-Pierre-le-Vieux, 6, place Saint-Pierre-le-Vieux
Daily 8.30am–7pm

Eight paintings by Henri Lützelmann depicting the Passion of Jesus decorate the choir of Saint-Pierre-le-Vieux. In one of them, a woman holds out a cloth imprinted with the face of Jesus. The scene refers to a little-known episode from the Passion, yet one that appears in many churches across the world (see opposite).

During the Revolution, the eight paintings were confiscated from Église Sainte-Madeleine in Strasbourg before being transferred to Saint-Pierre-le-Vieux.

The extraordinary story of Veronica's veil

Veronica's veil is one of the most complex and disputed relics in history. It is mentioned frequently in the history of art, and in many churches, there is a representation of a veil with the face of Christ printed on it – often discreetly for those unfamiliar with the legend. The origins of this cult can be found in the Gospels of Mark (5, 25-34), Matthew (9, 20-22) and Luke (8, 43-48), which recount the episode of a haemorrhoid (a woman who lost blood) who was healed by Jesus. Around the year 400, the Bishop of Lydia named her Berenike, shortly before the apocryphal Gospel of Nicodemus (6th century) finally gave her the name Veronica (or, depending on the Latin, Greek, Palaeoslav or Coptic languages, the names Vacilla, Balilla, Basilissa and Berenice). Since Veronica seems to derive from the Latin word *vera* (true) and the Greek *eikon* (image), meaning 'true image', the character of Veronica was gradually invented and gradually distinguished from that of the haemorrhoid. For others, the word comes from the Greek *pherenike*, meaning bearer (*phero*) of victory (*nike*). In the 7th century, another apocryphal text, Death of Pilate, speaks of Veronica as a confidante of Jesus, whom she asked for an image for when she was away from him. Christ then gave her the veil on which his face was printed. Around 1160, the canon of St Peter's in Rome, Pietro Mallius, theorised that this legend originated when, on her way to Golgotha, a woman removed her veil and placed it over Christ's face to wipe it clean, and that his face was miraculously imprinted. This hypothesis gained ground and gradually became accepted as the true story of this rare and miraculous image *achéropoiète* ('not made by the hand of man'). Veronica's veil is said to have had a troubled history. The earliest testimonies date from the 6th century, when the veil was seen in Ephesus, then in Camulia, a town that previously existed in the present-day region of Cappadocia, Turkey. In 574, on the orders of Emperor Justin II, the veil was transported to Constantinople before arriving in Rome in 705, in the Chapel of St Veronica in St Peter's Basilica, which Pope John VII had built. The relic then disappeared during the construction of the new basilica, between 1506 and 1608, or in 1527, during the sack of Rome. Some believe that the veil was actually brought from Rome to the small town of Manoppello, in Abruzzo, some 80 kilometres from Rome, where it can still be seen today.

Superimposing the Manoppello veil and the Turin Shroud would also have shown that the face printed on the two pieces of cloth belonged to the same man. Scientific studies have also shown that the veil was made from a fabric with extraordinary properties called *byssus* (sea silk, *bisso* in Italian). Made from fibres secreted by a bivalve mollusc (*Pinna nobilis*), byssus was historically the most precious fabric of Antiquity. Still produced by hand on the island of Sant'Antochio in south-west Sardinia, notably by Chiara Vigo, byssus is the only known material that lets light through, changes colour according to the illumination, does not dissolve in water, and is resistant to alcohol, ether, acid and fire.

THE LANSQUENET OF RUE DU FAUBOURG NATIONAL

14

Historical vestige related to the Poêle des Jardiniers

7, rue du Faubourg National
Tram A, C, D – Gare Centrale stop

Perched atop the building at 7, rue du Faubourg National in Strasbourg is a statue of a *lansquenet* (see opposite), a striking reminder of the city's rich corporate and military past.

This sculpture originally adorned the Poêle des Jardiniers (Gardeners' Taproom), a convivial gathering place and meeting hall for this influential city guild.

Their headquarters, built in 1600 in the Renaissance style, were destroyed during the siege of Strasbourg in 1870, when the neighbourhood suffered heavy bombardment.

In 1897–98, Jacques Krenker, the owner of a nearby brewery, constructed the current building on the same site in an 18th-century style, carefully preserving one remarkable element from the old structure: the lansquenet statue.

The presence of a lansquenet on the Poêle des Jardiniers might seem surprising for an agricultural guild, but it can be explained by several factors.

Firstly, guilds at that time were not limited to economic activities – they also played a role in the defence of the city. Gardeners, like other tradespeople, could be called upon to help protect Strasbourg, which justified the association with the lansquenet.

Secondly, the statue likely served as a symbol of prestige. Despite their modest professions, members of the gardeners' guild held full civic rights: they could vote, participate in city affairs and were fully integrated into the political and social life of Strasbourg. The image of the lansquenet reinforced their importance in the fabric of the city.

Lastly, lansquenets frequently took part in festivities organised by the guilds.

With their colourful uniforms and martial bearing, they added splendour to processions and parades, symbolising power and respectability.

Lansquenets: Renaissance mercenaries

By the 15th century, Europe's military landscape was undergoing profound change.

The rise of standing armies and the need for disciplined troops led to the emergence of lansquenets – Germanic mercenaries whose name comes from the German *Landsknecht* (servant of the land), a reference to their rural origins.

They rose to fame under Emperor Maximilian I of Habsburg, who employed them to counter the formidable Swiss pikemen. By the 16th century, lansquenets were fighting in conflicts across Europe, often under the banners of Francis I of France or Charles V of the Holy Roman Empire.

Their success was due to both their formidable armaments and their compact battlefield formations, capable of breaking enemy lines.

They wielded pikes up to five metres long, halberds, arquebuses and massive two-handed swords called *espadons*, reserved for the strongest among them.

Lansquenets dominated Renaissance battlefields, notably during the infamous sack of Rome in 1527 under Charles V.

But as military tactics evolved and national armies grew more professional, their influence waned. By the 17th century, they had largely vanished, replaced by modern, regimented troops.

Exuberant outfits to prove success and value

Lansquenets were hard to miss. Unlike heavily armoured knights, they favoured mobility, wearing flamboyant clothing: brightly coloured tunics, slashed sleeves and striped boots.

These extravagant outfits were not mere vanity – the more lavishly a lansquenet dressed, the more he demonstrated his success on the battlefield and his value as a mercenary.

PLAQUE ON EXECUTIONER'S TOWER

⑮

A building full of chilling memories

Quai Turckheim

Although the people of Strasbourg are familiar with the *Henckerturm* ('the Executioner's Tower'), which looks identical to the other towers close to the Covered Bridges, many are unaware of its sinister history. Yet a plaque affixed to its base, next to the Quai Turckheim, recalls the story.

In 1286, the Henckerturm was nicknamed *Stockhus*, the name of a wooden torture instrument in which convicts' feet were squeezed as in a press. The tower then acquired other names: 'the Tower of Chains' and 'the Tower of the Galley Slaves'. It was used until 1834.

Located at some remove from the Covered Bridges, it guarded the access to the Rue de la Fontaine (now called Rue Seyboth), which was an area of ill repute. In the 18th century, this street was successively nicknamed Rue du Bourreau ('Executioner's Street'), Rue du Glaive ('Broadsword Street'), Rue Ça ira ('That Will Do Street') and Rue des Pénitents ('Penitents' Street').

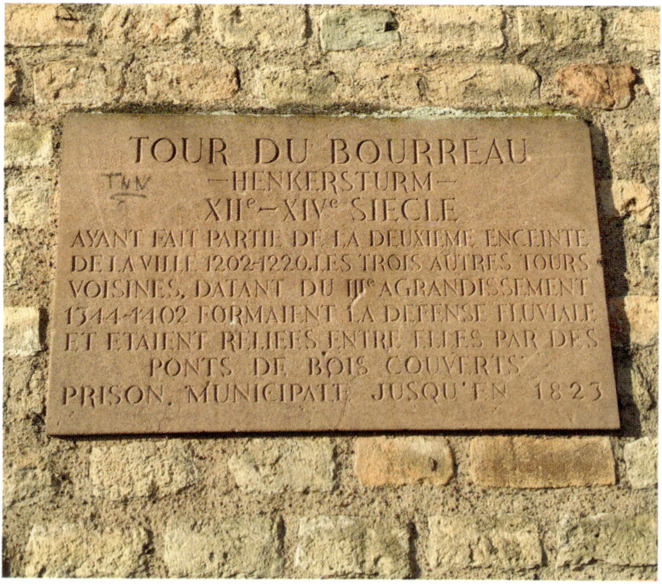

The origin of the 'Covered Bridges' name

In the neighbourhood of La Petite France, four towers were built between 1230 and 1250 (a fifth was destroyed by fire in 1869). They formed part of the first enclosure of stone fortifications in Strasbourg. Three of the towers stand on a bridge, and together they have retained their former name of 'Covered Bridges'. At the time of their construction, these bridges were made of wood, covered with roofs of the same material to protect the powder and weapons. Equipped with traffic tunnels leading into the city, they were closed to the outside and to possible assailants.

When Louis XIV visited the site in 1681, he considered this defence system obsolete and asked Vauban to design a modern system, which was implemented by the engineer Jacques Tarade (1640–1722). Since then, the towers have often been used as prisons.

The wooden Covered Bridges were demolished in 1748 and replaced by footbridges on stilts; the current stone bridges connecting the towers date from 1856. Despite the destruction of the original covered bridges, the system has kept this name and was listed as a Historic Monument in 1928.

The little-known names of the brick towers known as the 'Covered Bridges'

Passers-by are often unaware that the four brick towers of La Petite France have names, handed down by oral tradition: as the plaques on each of them specify, the first is called *Heinrichsturm* ('the Tower of the Lock-Keeper', or 'Heinrich's Tower'), the second *Hans von Altheimturm* ('the Tower of Hans – or Jean – of Altheim'), the third *Französische Turm* ('the French Tower') and the last *Stöckelsturm* or *Henkersturm* ('the Executioner's Tower').

Since Roman times, Strasbourg has been surrounded by fortifications to protect it from enemy invasions. Over the centuries, the growth of the city led to the destruction of towers and walls, which were rebuilt further afield, often using stones from the demolished structures. The city still retains some traces of its old enclosures, which include the towers of the Covered Bridges. The location was strategic at the time because the Ill, whose current runs from west to east, enters directly into the city here and divides into several branches to form a delta.

SCULPTURE OF A LANSQUENET WITH A DOG ⑯

A secret carved in stone

4, quai de la Bruche
Tram B, F – Alt Winmärik stop

© Tangopaso

At 4, quai de la Bruche, nestled on a 16th-century house, a discreet sculpture depicts a Lansquenet – a mercenary foot soldier from the Renaissance – accompanied by a small dog.

Beneath it is an inscription in German: *Das Haus stehet in Gottes Hant / Und ist zuom Dreibel Genant* ('This house is in the hands of God and is called The Grapes'). This seemingly anecdotal detail reveals an overlooked part of Strasbourg's history.

Built in 1599, the house once accommodated a famous inn, Zum Treibel ('The Grapes'), which was popular with sailors paying the *Wasserzoll* river toll before entering the city.

The sign was inspired by a huge walnut tree that stood nearby until it was destroyed by the harsh winter of 1704. Even today, a restaurant continues the tradition under the name Au Fantassin ('The Infantryman'), likely in reference to a former innkeeper.

But why depict a Lansquenet on the façade of an inn?

This soldier, easily recognised by his halberd and loose-fitting clothing, evokes a time when such mercenaries filled the armies of the Holy Roman Empire.

Strasbourg, as a border city and commercial hub, was well acquainted with these soldiers of fortune, who were both feared and respected. Their likeness on buildings served as both a tribute to their military role and a warning: a Lansquenet often marked a place under protection.

The sculpture itself is typical of the late Renaissance style.

Other Lansquenets in Strasbourg

There are two other sculptures of Lansquenets in the city: at 7, rue des Hallebardes (see p. 112) and 7, rue du Faubourg National (see p. 42).

For more on Lansquenets, see p. 43.

THE FORMER ICE HOUSES OF STRASBOURG

(17)

The industrial past of La Petite France

Le Régent Petite France hotel – 5, rue des Moulins
03 88 76 43 43 – accueil@regent-petite-france.com – glacest.org

Before the invention of the refrigerator, ice was a precious commodity in summer, and its production a major industrial concern.

In Rue des Moulins, the Le Régent Petite France hotel has preserved some of the original installations which recall that, for over a century, the power of water was used to produce cold and freeze water into blocks of ice, right in the heart of La Petite France.

In the hotel's entrance hall, historic valves remain visible and are highlighted by modern lighting.

Just off the ground-floor corridor (to the right of the reception), further preserved period elements suggest the operation of the former plant.

Thanks to the Ill River, which divides into four branches upstream, the area forms a natural delta.

It was here, on the site of two medieval mills – the Spitzmuehle and the Dünzenmuehle – that the former ice houses were installed in the early 20th century.

In 1897, shareholders of the brewers and butchers' company KlarEisWerke zur Dünzenmuehle bought the land from the millers who had long used the waterfalls for mechanical energy.

Their aim was to set up an ice house, which would allow for the storage of beer and meat, and to brew low fermentation beer.

Using electric turbines, the ice plant operated with considerable autonomy. By 1912, it could produce 120 tonnes of ice per day.

Details of this unique European industrial heritage site are impressive: the hydraulic turbines (one of 171 horsepower, two of 236) are fitted with 30-metre hemp ropes and a 64-metre main transmission axis.

Two wells 35 metres deep pumped drinking water to make ice, stored in three 240-cubic-metre basins (now gone).

The ice house ceased production definitively on 31 May 1990 due to lack of business.

How was ice stored before refrigerators?

Until the late 19th century, many European castles were equipped with ice houses – large underground pits or wells where winter ice from lakes and rivers was stored.

These structures were usually north-facing, insulated by earth mounds and masonry domes.

Inside, the ice was packed with straw and branches to reduce air flow.

To reduce air circulation, buckets of water were regularly poured into the gaps and the water solidified as it flowed, filling in the voids and compacting into a solid mass. Meltwater collected at the bottom of the pit was drained off via special cavities.

In Strasbourg, the cellars of the Palais des Rohan still house a spherical ice house of 5.70 metres in diameter (not open to the public). In the 18th century, ice was precious for preserving food, and the Palais des Rohan was able to contain up to 40 tons of it, a supply that could last for several years. It was used to preserve food, cool drinks and to make ice cream and sorbets throughout the year.

At Versailles, 13 royal ice houses were constructed under Louis XIII and Louis XIV.

There were 13 of them at the time: near the mills of Clagny, at the Potager, near the Menagerie, at Trianon, and in the Parc-aux-cerfs district, in Versailles itself. Today, only three remain: the first two, which are circular, are located on the grounds of the Petit Trianon, and the third is in Satory.

The underground, double-doored ice houses at Petit Trianon, installed in 1686, were still in use until 1909. To supply them, workers broke ice from the Grand Canal or Swiss pond using axes and mallets.

In the 19th century, breweries began to make extensive use of iceboxes, not only to preserve beer, but also, and above all, to produce it using bottom fermentation.

The ice trade flourished, particularly in the United States, where ice was shipped by rail and sea, revolutionising the food-processing industry.

From outside, on the downstream side of the Spitzmuehle, the turbine superstructures remain visible at the lock. The site is now listed as a Historic Monument and is only accessible to the public during the European Heritage Days in September.

La Petite France: a former open-air brothel which owes its name to syphilis, the 'French disease'

Although the charming Petite France neighbourhood, popular with tourists from around the world and listed as a UNESCO World Heritage site since 1988, is nowadays famed for its traditional timber-framed houses and canals, its nefarious reputation has been blotted out by most travel guides.

It used to be the poorest and most disreputable place in Strasbourg, where soldiers and prostitutes swarmed.

Strasbourg had been a garrison town since at least Roman times. And where there were soldiers, there were prostitutes ...

The authorities tried to drive the so-called *ribaudes* or 'swallows of the cathedral' (see p. 169) out of the city centre, to relocate them in this isolated and derelict district.

Rue du Bain-aux-Plantes – part of which is known as the Tanners' District – was lined with tanneries.

Evidence of this can still be seen in the oldest houses with their open attics for drying hides.

In 1687 a hospital for syphilis patients, then called *mal des Français* ('French disease'), was moved to 6, rue des Moulins and led to the area's enduring name.

Until the 19th century, Rue du Bain-aux-Plantes was cut off from the Saint-Thomas district by the Tanners' Ditch, which was only filled in after 1840 (see p. 21).

The founding in 1503 of the first hospice at Finkwiller (boundaries to the north and west the Ill river, to the east Rue de la Première Armée and to the south the Hôpital Civil) treated mercenaries returning from the Naples campaign of King Charles VIII of France, who brought back a new disease, syphilis.

Prostitutes, gradually driven from the cathedral, came to work here. By the 18th century the place was known as the 'Hôpital des Incurables'.

But Rue du Bain-aux-Plantes has more: the *bain* in question was home to a public bathhouse.

Although technically divided into male and female sections, in practice it was not uncommon for men and women to mingle in the same room.

Legend of the Finkwiller ghosts

It's said that a moaning washerwoman walks around the neighbourhood at nightfall, and plunges passers-by into the water until they drown. Her husband, a cooper, has also been spotted with her.

THE LOHKÄS' SIGN

(18)

Brewing alchemy and the memory of tanners in Strasbourg

25, rue du Bain-aux-Plantes
dna.fr/edition-de-molsheim-schirmeck/2015/09/23/les-lohkastreppler-de-barr
Trams A or D – Grand'Rue stop

Nestled in the heart of Petite-France, Lohkäs is much more than a traditional Alsatian restaurant.

On its half-timbered façade dating from the Renaissance, this house reveals a discreet, almost esoteric sign: a sign representing the brewers' star, framing an old cheese mold.

The brewers' star is an ancient symbol, used since 1397 in brewing communities throughout the Germanic world.

In Petite-France, formerly a working-class and artisan district, leather tanning was also a major activity.

The tanners used a vegetable mixture made from oak and chestnut bark (called *tannée*, or *Lohe* in Alsatian). After use, the remaining bark was packed into round molds without bottoms, fitted with handles: the famous cheese molds.

Frédéric Lix © DNA

The result, dried for months, was called *Lohkäs* ('tannin cheese'). This product, sold by a colorful local character, the *Lohkästreppler*, was not cheese but a domestic fuel, a sort of ancestor of the heating brick.

The name of the restaurant, located on the site of a former warehouse, pays tribute to this now forgotten practice, as well as to the neighborhood's ancient craftsmanship.

For more information on the brewers' star and its symbolism, see p. 289.

SCULPTURE OF A BEAR EATING A PRETZEL ⑲

The pretzel, an Alsatian symbol charged with meaning

98, Grand'Rue
Tram A, D – Grand'Rue stop

In the bustling streets of Strasbourg, a discreet detail steeped in history often escapes the notice of hurried passers-by. At 98 Grand'Rue, under the main window on the first floor, a sculpted bear holding a pretzel quietly bears witness to the city's artistic past.

Built in 1769 for the baker Jean Jung and his wife Catherine Simon, this house continued a baker's tradition that had lasted for centuries. Before the introduction of street numbers, carved signs and figures were used to identify businesses – which explains the placement of the bear eating a pretzel on the façade.

A bakery already stood at this spot as early as 1572. Its emblem, the sculpted bear, came from the name of a nearby inn, L'Ours Noir (The Black Bear), while the pretzel symbolised the baker's trade.

The word pretzel is a phonetic transcription of the German Brezel, itself derived from the popular Latin *brachitella*, from *bracchium* (arm). For some, its intertwined shape evokes crossed arms in prayer, suggesting a monastic origin (see opposite).

In Alsace, the pretzel is far more than a tasty snack – it's a symbol of love. In past centuries, during the New Year, young men would offer a large pretzel to the woman they admired. If she accepted it and shared it with him, it was a sign that she accepted him in happy union.

Origin of the pretzel

The pretzel is first recorded in 743 CE in Carolingian monastic culture. The 'Hortus Deliciarum' (Garden of Delights), a medieval pictorial encyclopaedia from the 12th century written at Hohenburg Abbey on Mont Sainte-Odile in Alsace, and the 'Chronica Majora', a 13th-century Latin illustrated manuscript held at Corpus Christi College, Cambridge, and the British Library in London, both depict pretzels.

According to legend, the pretzel was invented in 1477. A baker from the German Roman Empire, originally from Bouxwiller in Bas-Rhin, was imprisoned for under-baking his bread. He was sentenced to death. Allegedly, his wife pleaded with the king to give her husband one last chance. The king agreed, on the condition that the baker invent a bread 'through which the sun would shine three times' within three days.

While the baker was in his kitchen, desperately searching for inspiration, he noticed his wife through the window, kneeling in prayer with her arms crossed over her chest. That image sparked an idea: he twisted a strip of dough to mirror her posture, creating three holes through which the sunlight could pass, as required by the king.

Just before baking, their cat knocked over a container of baking soda used to clean the oven plates. With no time to make a new batch, the baker baked the pretzels as they were – unwittingly inventing the soft pretzel, which later became a symbol of prosperity and luck.

Another version of the story claims that a baker from Brescello, a small village in Emilia-Romagna, Italy, created the pretzel and named it after his hometown.

© Franzfoto

SCULPTURE OF PRINCESS EUROPA

20

A hidden sign loaded with symbolism

Hôtel de l'Europe
38, rue du Fossé des Tanneurs
Tram A, D – Langstross Grand'Rue stop – Homme de Fer stop

An unsuspected artistic treasure is hidden at 38, rue du Fossé des Tanneurs. A modest sculpture, tucked beneath a beam on the façade of the Hôtel de l'Europe (formerly the Hôtel de la Vignette), represents Princess Europa.

The building, dating from 1870, is typical of 19th-century architecture, with nine rows of windows spread across four storeys. Although the balconies on the first and second floors have since disappeared, a striking feature was added during the renovation of the façade in the 1990s: a female figure carved from local sandstone watches over the hotel entrance from a corbel above. Her serene expression, framed by flowing hair, and her gentle smile are captivating. The sphere she holds symbolises the transmission of knowledge and the expansion of European culture.

This sculpture, which also serves as a hotel sign, is a tribute to the legend of Europa and a direct reference to Greek mythology. According to legend, Princess Europa, daughter of the Phoenician King Agenor, was abducted by Zeus, king of the gods, who took the form of a tame white bull. Drawn to its gentleness, Europa climbed onto its back, only for the bull to carry her across the sea to the island of Crete. From their union came three sons, including Minos, the future Cretan king and founder of the labyrinth of the Minotaur. To honour Europa, Zeus gave her name to an entire continent: Europe.

The presence of this sculpture at the Hôtel de l'Europe is no coincidence. Strasbourg – a city at the crossroads of cultures and home to major European institutions – perfectly embodies the legacy of the mythological princess. This discreet, almost hidden decoration stands as a tribute to the transmission of European values and the enduring history of a civilisation rooted in ancient myths.

A POTTER'S EMBLEM

(21)

A discreet witness to this craft's history

81, Grand'Rue
Tram A, D – Grand'Rue stop

In the heart of Strasbourg's Grand'Rue, the entrance to No. 81 is topped by a sculpture of flowers in an earthenware vase – a discreet yet elegant symbol of the pottery trade once practised here.

Dating from the 17th century, the house was owned by various individuals, including the potter Jean Henri Fanck, who lived here between 1761 and 1785. In 1772, Fanck partially rebuilt the façade, removing the corbel, adding a ground floor entirely clad in sandstone, and inserting decorative bands between the three floors. He also had his personal emblem carved above the entrance, inscribed with '1 7 J H F 7 2' – marking the date of construction and his initials.

Though subtle, this ornamentation reflects the important role pottery once played in Strasbourg's daily life. The craft was central to the region's economy, especially at its peak in the 19th century, and the skills of local artisans helped shape the city's architectural heritage.

The place where Claude Rouget de Lisle composed the 'Marseillaise'

In the 18th century, this building was numbered 126 Grand'Rue. It was here that Claude Rouget de Lisle – then a captain of engineers stationed in Strasbourg – composed the famous war song of the Rhine Army on the night of 25 to 26 April 1792. Today, a plaque to the right of the door commemorates the event. Sung for the first time on 26 April in the parlour of Mayor Philippe Frédéric de Dietrich, the piece was originally a revolutionary call to arms against foreign invasion, composed just five days after France declared war on Austria.

It was both a patriotic anthem and a defiant cry for liberty against tyranny.

The song took the name 'La Marseillaise' in July of that year, when General Mireur, who had come to Marseille to organise the march of volunteers from the south, published it for the first time.

The Marseille federate troops adopted it as their marching song, performing it during their triumphant entry into the Tuileries in Paris on 30 July 1792.

The Parisian crowd immediately dubbed it 'La Marseillaise'. It was officially declared France's national anthem on 14 July 1795. The city of Strasbourg later honoured its composer by naming a major thoroughfare after him: Quai Rouget de Lisle.

CARVED ARTICHOKE AT FORMER HÔTEL DE LA MONNAIE

(22)

Symbol of a well-protected currency

Courtyard of École Saint-Thomas
2, rue de la Monnaie
Tram A, D – Grand'Rue stop

At 2, rue de la Monnaie, in the heart of Strasbourg, stands a discreet column in the courtyard of the former Hôtel de la Monnaie.

Topped by a carved relief in the form of an artichoke with finely detailed leaves arranged in superimposed crowns, it carries a wealth of fascinating historical meaning.

This rare motif in classical architectural ornament is deeply symbolic. Associated with prosperity and abundance, it reflects the financial nature of the site.

Although its use has changed, the former Hôtel de la Monnaie remains a symbol of Strasbourg's financial past, testifying to the city's importance to traders and merchants in both medieval and modern times.

The complex structure of the artichoke – with a heart protected by multiple layers – echoes the value of the coins once struck here and the care with which they were handled.

Other hypotheses suggest an allusion to trade between Strasbourg and Italy, where the artichoke had been a valuable commodity since the Renaissance. Some historians even detect a play on words or a humorous touch from the builders of the time.

First, there's the playful music of words. *Artichaut*, pronounced quickly in French, can sound like *Art y chaud* (Art is hot there) – a mischievous way of suggesting that art flourished here, full of ingenuity. It may also reference the activity of the mint itself, where precious metals were melted to create coins – a secret alchemy that transformed raw materials into wealth.

It can also be seen as a metaphor for currency: like an artichoke, with leaves guarding its tender heart, money is precious and often well protected. A parallel between vegetable and finance, discreetly carved in stone with humour.

Finally, there's visual irony: what could be more unexpected than an artichoke perched on a classical column at an official site? Perhaps a sly gesture from the stonemasons towards the strict rules of classical architecture – or a subtle reminder that behind great economic systems there's always room for a little mischief.

The history of artichokes

The artichoke is a Mediterranean plant derived from wild thistle. The earliest known cultivation dates back to ancient Egypt, and both the Greeks and Romans used it. Pliny the Elder even mentioned a similar vegetable in his writings. The plant almost disappeared during the Middle Ages but was reintroduced in Italy during the Renaissance. Its arrival in France is attributed to Catherine de' Medici, who brought it from Italy in the 16th century when she married Henri II. It soon became a refined delicacy enjoyed at the French court, particularly by Louis XIV, who loved and cultivated it at Versailles. The artichoke then spread to Spain, Provence and the Netherlands before being introduced to the Americas in the 18th century by French and Spanish settlers. Today, Italy, Spain and France are among the world's leading producers. A symbol of prosperity and abundance, beyond its association with wealth, the artichoke is also valued for its medicinal properties, especially for supporting liver function and aiding digestion. Over the centuries, the artichoke has crossed continents, becoming a culinary delicacy, a cultural symbol – and, in Strasbourg, an unusual decorative element!

Fig. 49. — **Artichaut** (*Cynara Scolymus*). — A Tête d'artichaut alors que les fleurs ne sont pas épanouies — B coupe verticale laissant voir la disposition des bractées qui forment l'involucre; le réceptacle charnu sur lequel elles s'insèrent ainsi que les fleurs encore en bouton — C le même fleuri — D l'un des fleurons — E sa coupe verticale — F fruit — G le même ayant perdu son aigrette — H coupe de ce fruit.

HEXAGRAMS OF THE ROSETTE AT ÉGLISE SAINT-THOMAS

(23)

The hexagram as a universal symbol

Place Saint-Thomas
Tram A, D – Grand'Rue stop

The rosette on the western façade of Saint-Thomas' church is a masterpiece of Rhenish Gothic-stained glass, dating from the late 13th or early 14th century.

Composed of 24 radiant compartments arranged around a central medallion, it illustrates the doubts of St Thomas, who questioned the Assumption of the Virgin in both body and soul.

Each compartment features a complex geometric design, often based on overlapping star or floral motifs. The dominant colours are ruby red, cobalt blue, silver yellow and opalescent white.

The patterns in the peripheral lobes are internal rosettes or six-pointed stars (hexagrams), symbolising the harmony of the created world.

The hexagram, a six-pointed star formed by the interlacing of two equilateral triangles – one pointing upwards, the other downwards – represents the spiritual and human nature of mankind.

Over time, it also became both a magical talisman and the emblem of the Hebrew religion.

For more on the hidden symbolism of the hexagram, see opposite.

The star hexagram: a magical talisman?

The hexagram – also known as the Star of David or the Shield of David – comprises two interlaced equilateral triangles, one pointing upwards and the other downwards. It symbolises the combination of man's spiritual and human nature. The six points correspond to the six directions in space (north, south, east and west, together with zenith and nadir) and also refer to the complete universal cycle of the six days of creation (the seventh day being when the Creator rested). Hence, the hexagram became the symbol of the macrocosm (its six angles of 60° totalling 360°) and of the union between mankind and its creator. If, as laid down in the Old Testament (Deuteronomy 6:4–9), the hexagram (mezuzah in Hebrew) is often placed at the entrance to a Jewish home, it was also adopted as an amulet by Christians and Muslims. So it is far from being an exclusively Jewish symbol. In both the Koran (38:32 et seq.) and 'The Thousand and One Nights', it is described as an indestructible talisman that affords God's blessing and offers total protection against the spirits of the natural world, the djinns. The hexagram also often appears in the windows and pediments of Christian churches, as a symbolic reference to the universal soul. The identification of Judaism with the Star of David began in the Middle Ages. In 1354 King Karel IV of Bohemia granted the Jewish community of Prague the privilege of putting the symbol on their banner. The Jews embroidered a gold star on a red background to form a standard that became known as the Flag of King David (*Maghen David*) and was adopted as the official symbol of Jewish synagogues. By the 19th century, the symbol had spread throughout the Jewish community. Jewish mysticism has it that the origin of the hexagram was directly linked with the flowers that adorn the *menorah*: irises with six petals. As well as offering protection, the hexagram was believed to have magical powers. This reputation originates in the famous Clavicula Salomonis (Key of Solomon), a *grimoire* (textbook of magic) attributed to Solomon himself but, in all likelihood, produced during the Middle Ages. The Clavicula contains a collection of 36 pentacles (themselves symbols rich in magic and esoteric significance) which were intended to enable communication between the physical world and the different levels of the soul. In Tibet and India, the Buddhists and Hindus read this universal symbol of the hexagram in terms of the creator and his creation, while the Brahmins hold it to be the symbol of the god Vishnu. Originally, the two triangles were in green (upright triangle) and red (inverted triangle). Subsequently, these colours became black and white, the former representing the spirit, the latter the material world.

MEDALLION OF GARLIC CLOVES

24

The patronym of the former owners

7, rue de l'Ail

Look closely above the entrance to no. 7, rue de l'Ail, and you'll spot a curious stone medallion: several garlic cloves tied together, carved in bas-relief.

In the 17th century, this site was home to the wine merchants' stove (see p. 87), once known as *Zum Knobloch*. Although *Knoblauch* means 'garlic' in German, the name had nothing to do with the pungent plant: it actually referred to the Knobelouch family, wealthy residents of the

street in the Middle Ages.

After the demolition of the stove in 1774, the garlic motif was added to the lintel, a visual pun on both the family name and the German word for garlic.

Garlic, a printer's mark

This building also once housed the Swiss-German printer Jean Knobloch, who died in 1528 (his birthdate is unknown).
Was it mere coincidence that he lived in a building so perfectly matched to his name, despite not inheriting the family home?
Knobloch trained with Martin Flach, one of Strasbourg's most prominent printers.
He gained citizenship rights in Strasbourg in 1501, following his marriage to the widow of his deceased employer, which enabled him to perpetuate his art for a long time to come.
When widowhood occurred within a guild, it was very common to find a bachelor among the craftsmen who was willing to remarry the widow.
He would then take charge of her and her children. The deceased husband's property also passed into the estate, and the tools of the trade remained in use within the guild.
He went on to print nearly 270 books, including around 200 in Latin and 70 in German.
He was also one of the first printers to produce in-8 (octavo) books in italics – volumes made by folding a sheet three times to form a 16-page booklet.
Knobloch's printer's mark? Naturally: a cluster of garlic cloves, featured in the colophons (the final notes of his books).

Gutenberg in Strasbourg

Gutenberg, born around 1400 in Mainz, spent roughly a decade in Strasbourg, beginning in 1434, where he perfected his technique for mechanically reproducing texts. Very few written records remain of this pivotal period, but it's likely that his work here sparked Strasbourg's rise as a major printing centre.
Gutenberg's first printed book – an incunabulum – was the celebrated 42-line Bible. Incidentally, the word 'Bible' comes from the Greek *biblion*, meaning 'book.'

HIDDEN FROG

(25)

A discreet but fun relief

6, rue de l'Épine
Tram A, D – Porte de l'Hôpital stop – Grand'Rue stop

In Strasbourg, at 6, rue de l'Épine, hidden from immediate view, a sculpted frog sits discreetly in a stone niche on the front of the house. Its legs are folded, its body slightly curved, and its round protruding eyes seem to observe passers-by with curiosity.

This is the last remnant of an old 'talking sign' dating from the 14th century – a reminder of a time when visual symbols were used to identify buildings before street numbers became common. It was not unusual for medieval sculptors to add playful features connected to Strasbourg, a city crossed by the River Ill and teeming with frogs and other batrachians.

A legal document from 1371 refers to this house by its historic name: *Zum güldenen Frosch* (With the Golden Frog), confirming its existence and identity since the 14th century. The date of 1691 engraved above the porch records a later partial reconstruction of the building.

Another detail of note: to the right of the frog, above the entrance to the building, a carved wreath of vine leaves and grape bunches recalls the presence of an old wine bar on the ground floor, once called *À la Grenouille*.

CARRIAGE DOOR AT 3, RUE DE L'ÉPINE

(26)

The only example of cartilage style in Strasbourg

3, rue de l'Épine
Tram A, D – Grand'Rue stop

In the alleys of Strasbourg's historic centre, at 3, rue de l'Épine, hides an architectural treasure often overlooked by hurried passers-by.

This carved wooden carriage door, with its sinuous volutes, organic forms and grimacing masks, recalls the Italian Mannerist ornaments of the late Renaissance. The sculpted details seem almost alive: dynamic curves unfurl while grotesque figures appear to scrutinise those who cross the threshold.

Look closely at the door and you will see that the undulating patterns strikingly resemble the cartilaginous structures and overall shape of the human ear.

This door is a rare and precious example of an ornamental style that has almost disappeared: the cartilage style, also known as the auricular style.

Dating from 1664 (although the building itself was remodelled in the 18th century), this *porte cochère* is the only surviving example of this exuberant style in Strasbourg.

Inspired by the rapidly evolving European decorative arts, the portal represents a transition between the classical harmony of the Renaissance and the emerging Baroque.

What is the cartilage style?

The cartilage, or auricular, style (*Ohrmuschelstil* in German, literally 'ear pavilion style'), is an ornamental decorative style that appeared in the late 16th century and flourished mainly in northern Europe during the first half of the 17th century.

Bridging Nordic Mannerism and the Baroque, it was particularly prominent in silverware but also applied to architectural elements such as doors, windows and frames, as well as a wide variety of decorative arts.

It is characterised by the use of abstract shapes whose resemblance to the side view of the human ear gives it its name.

The cartilage style then influenced Rococo ornamentation and later Art Nouveau.

RELIEF WITH THREE HARES

27

An ancient and mysterious motif

19, rue de l'Ail
Tram A, D – Porte de l'Hôpital stop – Grand'Rue stop

At 19, rue de l'Ail, an architectural detail often goes unnoticed by Strasbourg residents: a bas-relief sculpted on the pediment above the gate depicts three intertwined hares. Dated 1608, it marks the former presence of an inn named Aux Trois Lièvres ('At the Three Hares').

The house, now Regency in style and largely rebuilt in the 18th century, incorporated a neighbouring property called Zum Hasen ('At the Hare') in 1608, uniting the buildings under the same name.

The motif of the three intertwined hares is both universal and ancient, found in Europe and Asia since the Middle Ages. It relies on

an optical illusion: while three animals are always depicted, only nine legs are visible – each hare sharing a leg with another. Similar to the triquetra (see following double-page spread), it symbolises an eternal cycle, cosmic harmony and an ancestral mysticism often linked to reincarnation.

In Strasbourg, this relief recalls the local tradition of carved signs used to identify buildings before the introduction of street numbers. The design also resembles decorations on traditional Alsatian pottery, particularly that of Soufflenheim (featuring three hares and three ears).

Framed by scrollwork and decorative flourishes typical of the late Renaissance, the relief is carved from Vosges sandstone – a robust local stone that has survived the centuries despite the ravages of time and urban pollution.

Many interpretations exist for this motif. In medieval Christian art, the three hares evoke the Trinity; in European pagan beliefs, they represent renewal and the cyclical nature of life, rooted in the idea of reincarnation; in China, they are linked to the moon and the immortality of the soul.

Positioned above an old inn, this symbol could also have been intended to attract good fortune and prosperity, enticing travellers and passing merchants.

Symbolism of the triquetra (triskelion)

The triquetra (from Latin *triquetra*, meaning 'three angles', or Greek *triskelion*, meaning 'three legs') is a symbol formed by three intertwined arcs, creating a continuous figure without beginning or end.

A universal motif uniting different beliefs and traditions throughout history, its meaning centres on unity in diversity, endless cycles and protective power, making it a symbol of enduring fascination.

Often represented as three overlapping *vesica piscis* (fish bladders formed by intersecting circles), the triquetra is found in multiple civilisations with profound meanings linked to the cycles of life, harmony and interconnectedness.

The oldest representations appear in the megalithic temples of Malta, but it is more commonly associated with Celtic culture. For the Celts, it symbolised the Trinity in multiple forms: earth, air, water; or birth, life, death. It frequently adorned stones, jewellery and weapons, representing divine protection and eternity.

According to archaeologist Albert Grenier, the triquetra symbolised the sun for the Gauls, representing its three visible phases: morning, noon and dusk. It also reflected Celtic society's division into three main castes – bards and druids (spiritual power), kings (temporal power), and peasants/artisans (material power) – paralleling the theoretical organisation of Hindu society. The triquetra is thus considered the European equivalent of the Hindu swastika. This resemblance is perhaps unsurprising, as Celtic religious thought closely parallels Hinduism in its metaphysical foundations.

The triquetra is also associated with the triple goddess (Brigid, Morrigan), representing the three ages of womanhood: maiden, mother, crone.

With Christian influence, it later became a symbol of the Holy Trinity (Father, Son and Holy Spirit), appearing in religious art such as the 'Book of Kells' (8th century).

Since 1285, the flag of Sicily has featured a triskelion (triple spiral) with three bent legs rotating around a central human head – a symbol known as the Trinacria, representing the island's three capes.

In esoteric traditions, the triquetra is sometimes used as a symbol of protection. In alchemy, it represents the fundamental forces of nature and the unbroken cycle of life.

© Letazwiki

© Alain Van den Hende

STATUE OF THE KNIGHT LIEBENZELLER

(28)

The forgotten founder of the 'Free City of Strasbourg'

Place des Tripiers

On 16 April 2019, a 2.4-metre-high bronze statue by sculptor Christian Fuchs was unveiled in Place des Tripiers. It depicts knight Reimbold Liebenzeller (1225–1282) holding a crossbow. The inscription reads: 'Knight Liebenzeller – Winner of the Battle of Hausbergen – Father of the Free City of Strasbourg – 1262.' Another plaque beneath bears a quotation attributed to him before the decisive battle on 8 March 1262: 'Fight courageously and fearlessly for the honour of our city today, to perpetuate our freedom and that of our children and descendants.'

The statue commemorates a key but often overlooked moment in Strasbourg's history – the clash between a volunteer city army led by Liebenzeller and the troops of Bishop Walter de Geroldseck (1231–1263).

Upon becoming bishop in 1260, Geroldseck sought total authority over Strasbourg's ruling classes, imposing severe constraints and blockading the city.

On 8 March 1262, at the foot of Hausbergen hill, 300 knights and 6,000 infantrymen under Geroldseck were defeated by Liebenzeller's forces, who famously ordered the slaughter of horses to bring down the armoured knights. The bishop's forces retreated under a hail of arrows and bolts, and Geroldseck fled to Molsheim.

Strasbourg then became a Free Imperial City under the Holy Roman Empire, retaining its independence until annexation by France in 1681. Its municipal system remained unchanged until the French Revolution.

As there are no surviving portraits of Liebenzeller, Fuchs based the statue on contemporary descriptions. Although the crossbow played a vital role in the battle, the knight himself likely did not wield one, as it was deemed inappropriate for his rank.

INSCRIPTION ON THE FORMER 'POÊLE DE LA MAURESSE' FAÇADE

(29)

An historical error

7, rue du Vieux Marché aux Poissons

At number 7, Rue du Vieux Marché aux Poissons, stands à large building transformed in the 17th and 18th centuries. The site originally housed a 14th-century building named Zum Hern Moerlin ('Home of Sieur Moerlin').

Over time, the name was corrupted to Zur Moerin ('At the Mauresse's'), leading to a mistaken association with a Black servant. In fact, the name refers to Moerlin's coat of arms, which features a Moor's head – not an actual person (see photo).

A plaque on the building describes the site as the 'Poêle de la Mauresse,' or the stove of the Mauresse guild – one of many historical corporate meeting halls in Strasbourg.

By the 14th century, the guild housed here was unusually diverse, including: Salt and cured meat merchants, Fruit sellers, Candle makers, Rope makers, Tobacco processors, Cobblers, Rag dealers, Carters.

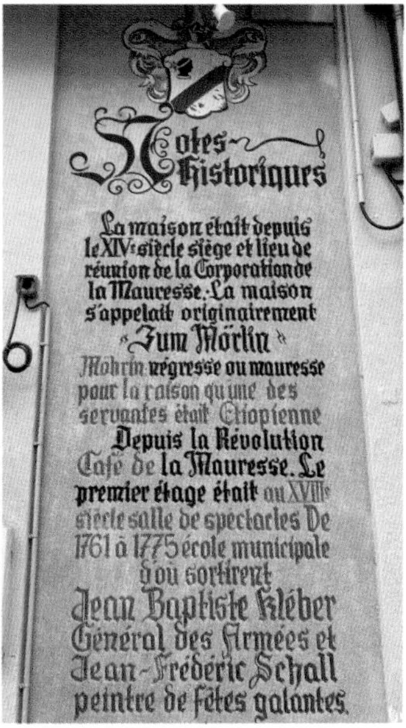

After the French Revolution, the Mauresse stove was repurposed as a drawing school, and later, in the 19th century, became a performance hall.

For many years, it was also home to a fish restaurant named La Mauresse.

For more information on stoves and guilds, see page 87.

FRESCOES ON THE FIRST FLOOR OF THE FORMER PHARMACIE DU CERF (30)

Undoubtedly Europe's oldest pharmacy

10, place de la Cathédrale and 11, rue Mercière
Ground floor freely accessible every day from 10am–8pm
First floor open during the European Heritage Days
To support local artisans, the municipality of Strasbourg – now the owner of the building – offers 11-month, generally non-renewable leases to local traders
Trams A, D – Grand'Rue stop

To support local artisans, the municipality of Strasbourg—now the owner of the building – offers 11-month, generally non-renewable leases to local traders: strasbourg.eu/une-vitrine-au-coeur-de-strasbourg.

The timber-framed Renaissance building facing Notre-Dame Cathedral at the corner of Rue Mercière is not only a fine example of Alsatian architecture but also the site of one of Europe's oldest pharmacies. Listed as a Historic Monument in 1929, it housed a pharmacy for centuries, which finally closed in 2000.

Since then, the ground floor has been used by pop-up shops and displays several sketches with medieval inspiration depicting the apothecary's profession. These were painted around 1900 by the Strasbourg artist Léo Schnug (1878–1933), who also decorated the nearby Maison Kammerzell (see p. 122). The first floor, open to the public only during the European Heritage Days, features a beautiful cycle of grisaille frescoes arranged in friezes. These illustrate the first Psalm of King David from the Bible, divided into eight scenes depicting 'obedience to God's law, which leads to salvation, and its refusal, which leads to corruption.' The artist's name remains unknown, though the work dates from the 16th century.

The first dispensary in this building was founded around 1268 by an apothecary named Heinrich Philippi. The pharmacy, which only became known as Zum Hirschen ('Du Cerf') in the mid-17th century, remained in operation under the direction of several successive families.

The building itself was gradually transformed between the 14th and 16th centuries, with its upper floors completed in 1567. It consists of three adjoining houses, two of which are connected under a single roof.

Three other pharmacies have laid claim to the title of Europe's oldest, but all were founded later than 1268: the Franciscan monastery of the Friars Minor in Dubrovnik (Croatia) dates from the early 14th century, while those of the Town Hall in Tallinn (Estonia) and Llívia (French Cerdanya) date back to the 15th century.

BIBLIOTHÈQUE PYTHAGORE

31

A rich humanist library

2, rue des Hallebardes
pythagore.asso@gmail.com
Saturday, 3pm–5pm

Few residents of Strasbourg are aware of the Bibliothèque Pythagore, despite its central location at number 2, rue des Hallebardes.

Run by volunteers (and self-funded through memberships and training courses), the Bibliothèque Pythagore offers a remarkable collection of more than 8,000 books, all focusing on humanism in its broadest sense. The collection ranges from spirituality to philosophy, Buddhism to Christianity, yoga to gnosis, Martinism to the Kabbalah, and Freemasonry to alchemy. All subjects concerning the intimate knowledge of the individual can be explored here.

The library was founded in 1920, when Strasbourg philanthropist Marthe North-Siegried (1866–1939) financed an association called Pythagore, which she enriched with valuable books. This wealthy widow, from a family of jewellers, was drawn to theosophical ideas – then fashionable – which answered her 'need for universal brotherhood' and simplicity of life.

Originally affiliated with the Theosophical Society – an association founded in New York in 1875, whose fundamental principle is that 'there is no religion higher than truth' – the library continues to uphold the precepts of Socrates. His famous quotation appears on the temple of Apollo at Delphi: 'Know thyself and thou shalt know all the mysteries of the Gods and of the Universe.'

Marthe North-Siegried

Born into a wealthy family of jewellers, Marthe North-Siegried (1866–1939) funded numerous charitable and humanitarian initiatives. She was behind the first vegetarian restaurant in Strasbourg, opened in 1930 on Rue de la Haute Montée, and the Society for the Protection of Animals, located on Rue de la Montagne Verte.

A devoted Francophile, she also worked to support prisoners of the First World War, regularly sending them care packages.

Today, she is best remembered for her role as president of the Association des Dames Françaises and her contributions to the Red Cross. In recognition of her efforts, she was awarded the Reconnaissance Française in 1920.

STATUE OF MADAME ROGER

32

A beautiful declaration of love

Corner of Place Gutenberg and 89, rue des Grandes Arcades

Look up at the corner of Place Gutenberg and 89, rue des Grandes Arcades, and you'll spot a statue of a woman at first-floor level, accompanied by a reference in pseudo-Gothic gold lettering to the 'Maison Roger.'

This discreet tribute recalls the Jean Roger jewellery store, which occupied the premises until 2017. The new owners have preserved its façade, a touching testimony to a beautiful love story.

Legend has it that the jeweller and watchmaker Jean Roger, inconsolable after the loss of his beloved wife during an Allied bombing raid in 1944 (see box below), commissioned this representation of her in her honour.

When the shop was rebuilt in 1955 by Strasbourg architect Érasme Schwab (1907–1974), Roger enlisted local sculptor Alphonse Rompel (1895–1961), a master at the Œuvre Notre-Dame, to create a life-sized statue.

The female figure, crafted by Rompel, is dressed in the style of the Rhine basin during the 16th century – when the building housed a bakery.

She wears an elaborate headdress, intricately embroidered, which frames her flowing hair. In her left hand, she holds a jewellery box containing a necklace of fine pearls, while with her right, she delicately places gold nuggets or precious stones on a tiny set of scales.

The Allied bombardments on 11 August 1944

The Allied bombardments on the afternoon of 11 August 1944 killed around 1,000 Strasbourg residents and destroyed 20 per cent of the city's buildings. The area around Place Gutenberg and Rue des Grandes Arcades was particularly devastated. Even the cathedral was struck, suffering damage to the Klotz Tower.

The affair of the Queen's Necklace: the role of the city of Strasbourg

In 1772, Louis XV wished to offer an incomparable diamond necklace to the countess du Barry (1743–1773). The piece was commissioned from the Parisian jewellers Boehmer and Bassenge. However, the creation process proved lengthy, particularly in gathering the required stones, as this 2,840-carat necklace was composed of numerous large diamonds set in an elaborate arrangement. Louis XV died in 1774, before the gift could be delivered.

Having invested heavily in the project, the jewellers attempted several times to sell the necklace to Marie-Antoinette, who had become Queen of France upon the accession of her husband, Louis XVI.

She refused repeatedly – partly because she had viewed Madame du Barry as a rival during her years as dauphine.

Madame de La Motte (Jeanne de Valois-Saint-Rémy, 1756–1791) then sought to insinuate herself at court. Facing chronic financial difficulties, she persuaded Cardinal Louis-René-Édouard de Rohan (1734–1803), Prince of Rohan and Bishop of Strasbourg,

to purchase the necklace. Rohan, a former ambassador to Vienna with a reputation for a dissolute lifestyle, had fallen out of favour with the Queen.

Eager to return to her good graces – especially as Madame de La Motte's lover, a skilled forger, had been sending him letters he believed were from Marie-Antoinette – he agreed.

In 1785, another forged letter prompted the Cardinal to pay 1,600 livres for the necklace, which he handed over to Madame de La Motte.

The swindlers promptly dismantled the piece, damaging the stones and selling them off in Paris, London and Brussels.

When the King discovered the affair, he had the Cardinal imprisoned in the Bastille for having conducted such a transaction under the Queen's name. Rohan was not permitted to return to his Strasbourg diocese until 1788.

The 'affair' significantly contributed to the fall of the Ancien Régime.

Given the Queen's reputation for extravagance, the public never believed that she had not been involved. The scandal became a symbol of the perceived excesses of the aristocracy, fuelling the anger that would soon erupt in revolution.

© Château de Breteuilsha

INSCRIPTION OF THE TRIBE OF MERCHANTS

33

Bearing witness to the former corporation of the Tribe of Merchants, known as the Tribe of the Mirror

5, rue Gutenberg

At number 5, rue Gutenberg, a discreet inscription engraved on the façade reads : 'Tribu des marchands –MDCCLXXXV' (1785) This marks the former meeting place of the Tribe of Merchants, also known as the 'Tribe of the Mirror.'

The name originates from the guild's original meeting place – a house called Zu dem Spiegel ('mirror' in German), mentioned as early as 1367. The original guild house, or 'stove', was rebuilt in the 18th century in Louis XV style and features a rare architectural configuration : three façades facing Rue du Miroir, Rue des Serruriers, and Rue Gutenberg.

NEARBY

Tobacco leaves on the balcony of the Tribe of Merchants

On the façade of number 5, rue Gutenberg, just beneath the inscription of the former Tribe of Merchants, the balcony is subtly adorned with tobacco leaves – a decorative tribute to one of Alsace's key 18th-century crops, which played a major role in the region's economic growth.

The stove : the house occupied by a trade guild

In Alsace, the term 'stove' referred to the guild house, or 'tribe', where the head office of a trade corporation was located. The name derives from the heated meeting room inside – known as the *Stub*, a wood-panelled, stove-warmed space common in Alsatian homes. By extension, *Stube* came to mean the main living room in Alsatian households, and eventually gave rise to the names of the region's typical taverns: the *Winstube* (wine tavern) and *Bierstube* (beer tavern).

UNDERGROUND ROMAN TOWER ON RUE DES GRANDES ARCADES

34

Well-hidden remains under a supermarket

Auchan Kléber supermarket
47–49, rue des Grandes Arcades
Exceptional visits by request (ask store management) :
03 88 32 51 53

In 1906, archaeologists uncovered the remains of a Roman defence tower in the basement of what is now the Auchan Kléber supermarket. Today, the structure – used as a storage area – is only accessible through special request.

Built between the late 3rd and early 4th centuries, the semi-circular tower measures 7.5 metres in diameter and 3.5 metres in height. It was part of the fortified camp of Argentorate (the Roman name for Strasbourg), and was officially listed as a Historic Monument in 1920.

Constructed with a wooden framework, the interior of the tower was filled with sandstone and limestone rubble – many stones recycled from earlier monuments, including funerary steles bearing Latin inscriptions.

The holes still visible in the structure once held wooden beams arranged in two levels – vertical and transverse – spaced about a metre apart. This criss-cross system formed what is known in Latin as opus spicatum (herringbone work).

The city of Strasbourg (then Argentorate) was originally a Roman fortified camp, constructed by a legion around 12 BCE. It formed a 19-hectare quadrilateral on the Grande Île, protected by the waters of the Ill and the Bruche – natural barriers to enemies crossing the Rhine.

Over time, successive walls were added to reinforce the camp's defences, and archaeologists have identified three distinct construction phases. To date, remains of 16 other similar semi-circular towers have been discovered in Strasbourg. Most are incorporated into existing buildings – particularly in the area around Place du Temple-Neuf – or buried in inaccessible cellars. The tower beneath the Auchan supermarket is the only one that is publicly visible.

The axis of Rue du Dôme and Rue des Hallebardes

Roman military camps and cities were built around two main intersecting streets: the *cardo* (north–south) and the *decumanus* (east–west). These axes remain visible today in the form of Rue du Dôme (*cardo*) and Rue des Hallebardes (*decumanus*).

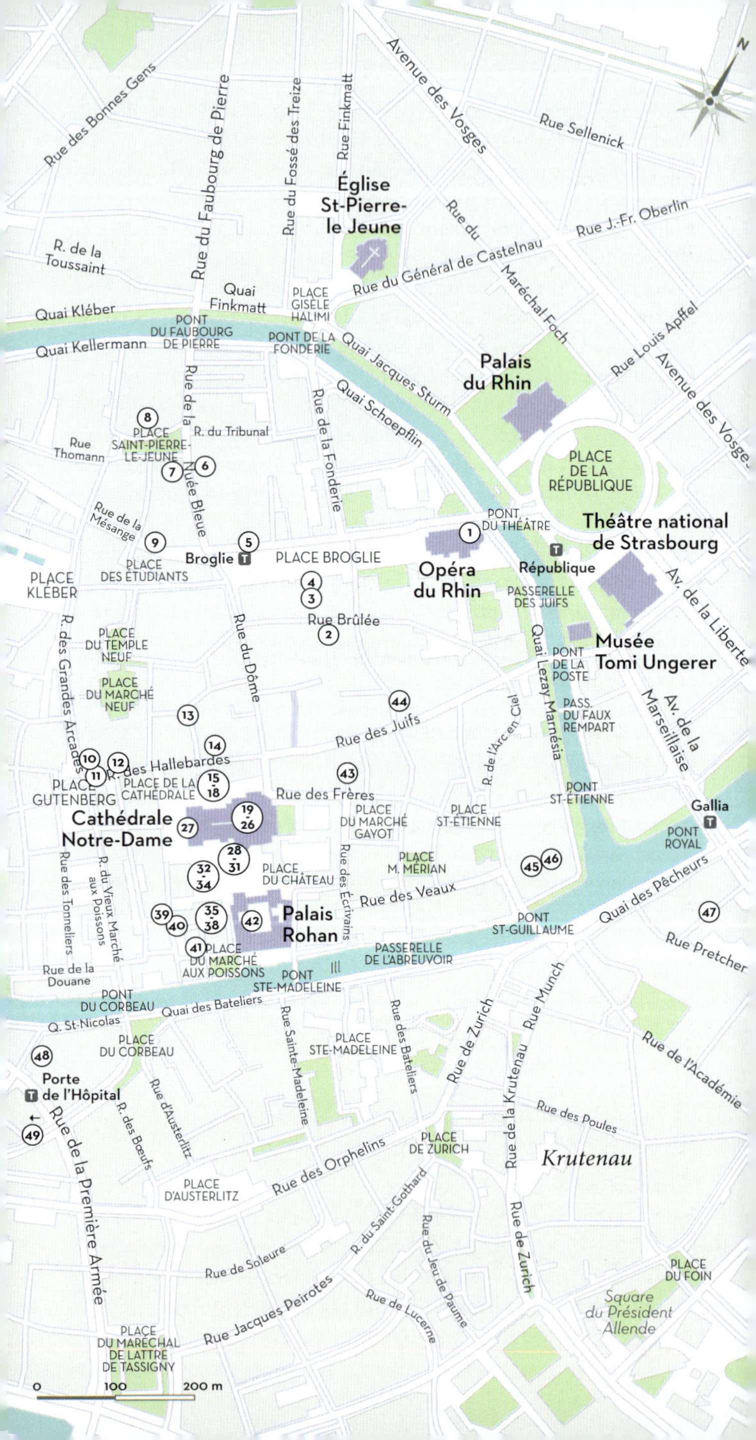

Église St-Pierre-le Jeune
Palais du Rhin
PLACE DE LA RÉPUBLIQUE
Théâtre national de Strasbourg
Opéra du Rhin
République
Musée Tomi Ungerer
Broglie
PLACE BROGLIE
PLACE KLÉBER
PLACE DES ÉTUDIANTS
PLACE SAINT-PIERRE-LE-JEUNE
PLACE DU TEMPLE NEUF
PLACE DU MARCHÉ NEUF
PLACE GUTENBERG
PLACE DE LA CATHÉDRALE
Cathédrale Notre-Dame
PLACE DU CHÂTEAU
Palais Rohan
PLACE DU MARCHÉ AUX POISSONS
PLACE DU MARCHÉ GAYOT
PLACE ST-ÉTIENNE
PLACE M. MÉRIAN
Gallia
PONT ROYAL
PONT ST-GUILLAUME
PASSERELLE DE L'ABREUVOIR
PONT STE-MADELEINE
PONT DU CORBEAU
PLACE DU CORBEAU
Porte de l'Hôpital
PLACE STE-MADELEINE
PLACE DE ZURICH
Krutenau
PLACE D'AUSTERLITZ
PLACE DU FOIN
Square du Président Allende
PLACE DU MARÉCHAL DE LATTRE DE TASSIGNY
Rue des Bonnes Gens
Rue du Faubourg de Pierre
Rue du Fossé des Treize
Rue Finkmatt
Avenue des Vosges
Rue Sellenick
Rue du Maréchal Foch
Rue J.-Fr. Oberlin
Rue du Général de Castelnau
R. de la Toussaint
Quai Finkmatt
PLACE GISÈLE HALIMI
Quai Kléber
Quai Kellermann
PONT DU FAUBOURG DE PIERRE
PONT DE LA FONDERIE
Quai Jacques Sturm
Quai Schoepflin
Rue Louis Apffel
Rue de la Nuée Bleue
R. du Tribunal
Rue Thomann
Rue de la Fonderie
Rue de la Mésange
PONT DU THÉÂTRE
PASSERELLE DES JUIFS
Av. de la Liberté
Rue Brûlée
R. des Grandes Arcades
Rue du Dôme
PONT DE LA POSTE
Quai Lezay Marnésia
PASS. DU FAUX REMPART
Av. de la Marseillaise
Rue des Juifs
R. de l'Arc en Ciel
R. des Hallebardes
PONT ST-ÉTIENNE
Rue des Frères
Rue des Écrivains
Rue des Veaux
Quai des Pêcheurs
Rue Pretcher
Rue des Tonneliers
R. du Vieux Marché aux Poissons
Rue de la Douane
Quai des Bateliers
Q. St-Nicolas
Rue Sainte-Madeleine
Rue des Bateliers
Rue de Zurich
Rue Munch
Rue de l'Académie
Rue de la Krutenau
Rue des Poules
Rue de la Première Armée
R. des Boeufs
Rue d'Austerlitz
Rue des Orphelins
R. du Saint-Gothard
Rue du Jeu de Paume
Rue de Soleure
Rue Jacques Peirotes
Rue de Lucerne
0
100
200 m
N

Centre East

SYMBOLS ON THE FOUNTAIN OF JANUS (1)

An apparent 'ruin,' one face turned to the future, the other to the past

Square Markus-Botzaris, to the north of the Opéra du Rhin Corner of Place Broglie and the Quai Schoepflin

Passing in front of the fountain of Janus, near the Opéra du Rhin, many passers-by assume it to be a fragment of an aqueduct from Roman times. However, this is not the case: this fountain, whose real name is 'La Naissance de la Civilisation' ('The birth of civilisation'), was designed by the Strasbourg artist Tomi Ungerer (1931–2019).

Built by the architect Paul Ziegler and the sculptor Denis Roth, this surprising work was inaugurated on 18 November 1988. A plaque also indicates the names of the three artists and mentions the presence of the Senator-Mayor Marcel Rudloff, as well as the Strasbourg 2000 Committee, at the inauguration.

The creation of the fountain was one of the events marking the celebration of the 2,000th anniversary of the city of Strasbourg. To symbolise the arrival of the new millennium, the figure chosen was the Roman god of beginnings and endings, of choices, of passages and of doors: Janus, with two faces, is represented with one face turned to the past and the other to the future.

Here, Janus also represents the city's dual Franco-German identity: one face looks towards the historic centre, the other towards the Neustadt.

This (fake) fragment of aqueduct, made of 5,000 bricks on a reinforced concrete structure, also evokes the Roman origins of the city (even though no aqueduct has been found in Strasbourg). One side bears the inscription 'Argentoratum MM' (Argentoratum being the Latin name of Strasbourg), and the other, 'Strasbourg 2000.'

Finally, the bricks of this three-pillar structure also reference the activity of Strasbourg's ancient brickworks.

Its 80-square-metre pool allows water to flow during the summer months.

One of the borders of the original Roman camp was located near the present-day fountain of Janus. The city took on its present name in 590, when Grégoire de Tours (538–594) referred to it as *Strateburgum*. It is generally agreed that the foundation of the city can be traced back to the reign of the emperor Augustus. In the year 12 BCE, the Roman legions of General Drusus entered the Grande Île. This village of Celtic fishermen then became known as Argentoratum.

BUST OF GUSTAVE STOSKOPF ②

A fundamental, little-known figure in the artistic history of Strasbourg

6, rue Brûlée

High above a plaque bearing his name, the bust of Gustave Stoskopf stands in a niche on the façade of no. 6, rue Brûlée. Today, few tourists or locals know who he was – yet he was a pivotal figure in the artistic and cultural history of Strasbourg.

Born in 1869 in Brumath, Gustave Stoskopf – whose surname means 'the pushed head' – began painting around 1886, training in Paris and later in Munich before returning to his native Alsace.

A prolific artist, Stoskopf produced numerous paintings and drawings, often portraying Alsatians in everyday life.

But he also excelled in other artistic fields, writing around 15 plays, including the famous 'Herr Maire' (see below), written in the Alsatian dialect.

More than just an artist, Stoskopf played a vital role in preserving and promoting Alsatian culture, which he feared was in danger of vanishing. To this end, he founded the Musée Alsacien in 1903 and, in 1905, opened the Maison d'Art Alsacienne – housed in the very building where his bust now stands.

The Maison d'Art Alsacienne was a permanent exhibition space that brought together artists, patrons, and collectors.

As a flagship of the Alsatian artistic revival, it helped introduce the ideas of Art Nouveau into Strasbourg's artistic scene, then viewed as rather stagnant.

Alongside fellow polymath Charles Spindler, Stoskopf showcased furniture and decorative pieces that were true works of art.

He also served as the director of a newspaper and was an energetic supporter of numerous literary and artistic societies, including the influential Revue Alsacienne Illustrée.

'Herr Maire'

In 1898, Stoskopf also founded the Théâtre Alsacien de Strasbourg. It was for this venue that he wrote 'Herr Maire', a comic and satirical play completed in just three weeks. The story follows the bumbling mayor of a village in Kochesberg (a region in the Lower Rhine) and a sly peasant who switches allegiance between France and Germany depending on who's in charge – reflecting the divided loyalties following Alsace's annexation by Germany in 1871. The comedy was filmed in 1939 and later banned by the Nazis. The play was an instant success, and remains a staple of Alsatian theatre to this day.

THE KUFRA OATH ON THE WAR MEMORIAL

3

'Swear not to lay down arms until our colours, our beautiful colours, fly over Strasbourg Cathedral'

Place Broglie
Near the Opéra du Rhin

At Place Broglie, near the Opéra du Rhin, stands a memorial engraved with an inscription that often goes unnoticed. It recalls the achievements of Colonel Philippe Leclerc de Hauteclocque (1902–1947), one of the key military leaders of Free France during the Second World War, and among the first officers to join General de Gaulle after the Appeal of 18 June 1940. Leclerc notably commanded the famous 2nd Armoured Division (2e DB), which went on to liberate Strasbourg.

As this memorial reminds us, Leclerc secured victory on 2 March 1941 over Axis forces (mainly Italian) in the Libyan oasis of Kufra. It was after this battle that he asked his soldiers to take an oath: 'Swear not to lay down arms until our colours, our beautiful colours, fly over Strasbourg Cathedral.'

The Kufra oath was fulfilled on 23 November 1944. Racing to relieve besieged Strasbourg with his five columns, Leclerc caught the enemy by surprise that morning. By evening, a makeshift French flag – with red fabric taken from a Nazi banner – had been raised atop the cathedral by Maurice Lebrun of the Moroccan Spahi Regiment.

The city, encircled by enemy troops, was subsequently defended by the Alsace-Lorraine Brigade and the French Forces of the Interior, who held Strasbourg until May 1945. While the siege itself did not see heavy combat, the symbolic significance was immense.

As for Leclerc and his distinguished division, they did not lay down their arms after Strasbourg's liberation, contrary to what might be suggested by the wording of the Kufra oath. The 2e DB, which had also been the first Allied unit to enter Paris on 24–25 August 1944, pushed on to Berchtesgaden in Bavaria. Between 4–5 May 1945, it was the first division to enter Hitler's secondary residence, the Berghof, and likely the nearby Kehlsteinhaus – the notorious 'Eagle's Nest.'

Leclerc died in a plane crash in 1947 and was posthumously awarded the rank of Marshal of France.

Incidentally, the famous French actor Jean Gabin volunteered to join the French Armed Forces in 1943 and, as a commander in the 2e DB, took part in the capture of Berchtesgaden.

'LA MARSEILLAISE' MONUMENT ④

The French national anthem was composed in Strasbourg

Banque de France
3, place Broglie
Local town hall, at the corner of Rue de la Comédie and Place Broglie
Rue de la Mésange
126, Grand'Rue

Despite its name, 'La Marseillaise' was composed in Strasbourg. Two sites on Place Broglie honour this fact: a commemorative plaque and a monumental statue.

The plaque on the Banque de France indicates that it was here that Claude Joseph Rouget de Lisle (1760–1836), a captain of engineers stationed in Strasbourg, first performed the anthem during a reception on 26 April 1792.

The event was hosted at the mansion of Philippe-Frédéric de Dietrich (1748–1793), the city's then-mayor.

The 'La Marseillaise' monument, next to the town hall, shows two soldiers holding the French flag, beneath the inscription 'Allons enfants de la Patrie' ('Arise, children of the Fatherland').

Created in 1922 by Alfred Marzolff (1867–1936), the statue was destroyed by the Nazis in 1940 and reconstructed in 1980 using a 1919 plaster model preserved by the Museum of Modern and Contemporary Art.

The two medallions showing Rouget de Lisle and Baron de Dietrich were salvaged from the monument's original base and now appear on the Banque de France façade.

'War Song for the Army of the Rhine'

Originally titled 'War Song for the Army of the Rhine', 'La Marseillaise' was written in support of French troops, following France's declaration of war against the King of Hungary and Bohemia on 20 April 1792.

According to tradition, Rouget de Lisle composed the anthem in a single night at his home on Rue de la Mésange – or possibly at 126 Grand'Rue – at Baron de Dietrich's request.

Blending popular musical motifs of the day, the song quickly gained popularity.

It was taken up by volunteers from Marseille, who marched to Paris to participate in the Fête de la Fédération.

Their association with the song led it to be known as 'La Marseillaise', which was adopted as the official national anthem

JEAN-MARIE KRAUTH'S 'LES BOUSSOLES'

⑤

Travel stops far beyond Strasbourg

On the floors of the 24 tram stations on Line B

Hidden beneath the feet of commuters at the 24 tram stations along Line B, 'Les Boussoles' ('The Compasses') is an art installation by Jean-Marie Krauth. Its discreet placement and lack of signage make it a little-known work, often overlooked by passers-by.

Installed in 2000 as part of the tramway extension, the artist embedded 12-centimetre Finnish Suunto compasses into the flooring of each platform. Each compass is set in an airtight, cylindrical bronze casing, protected by a glass window for visibility. Around each disc, an inscription indicates a geographical direction and a specific place, suggested by local residents – enigmatic destinations softly inviting us to travel.

Krauth's aim is to playfully disrupt our sense of direction by, for example, having a compass point north 180°, effectively indicating south.

The chosen materials interact with light and time. The bronze slowly oxidises, while the steady tread of feet polishes the glass to a smooth finish. With each passing day, the discs become more integrated into the fabric of the city, their sheen shifting with the weather.

Their seemingly random placement evokes the feeling of organised chaos, reflecting the countless trajectories that intersect within an urban space.

With 'Les Boussoles', Jean-Marie Krauth reminds us of a universal truth: we are constantly in motion in a city that itself is a place of passage, where each individual follows their own unique path – whether physical, spiritual, or imaginary. He invites us to shift our perspective, to lower our gaze and become fully present in our surroundings, perhaps even prompting us to redefine our own route.

THE ROOSTER ON RUE DE LA NUÉE BLEUE

⑥

A discreet detail steeped in history

11, rue de la Nuée Bleue
Tram B, C – Broglie stop

At 11, rue de la Nuée Bleue, an architectural curiosity catches the eye of even the most observant passers-by: a metal rooster mounted on the façade, which crows every day at noon. This decorative yet symbolic feature holds a fascinating story linked to some of Strasbourg's most significant historical events.

The rooster, designed with a mechanism that allows it to move and crow, is finely crafted with meticulous details on its feathers and comb, giving it a lifelike appearance. Positioned to overlook the street, it seems to watch over the surroundings like a vigilant guardian of time and history.

Opposite, at 12, rue de la Nuée Bleue, a hen symbolically responds to the rooster. This whimsical interaction between the two birds adds a playful touch for those who happen to notice.

The choice of the rooster was no accident. Installed in 1920, during the period of post-war reconstruction, the sculpture represents the Gallic rooster – a traditional emblem of France symbolising vigilance, pride and resilience. The piece was created by a mechanic working for Dernières Nouvelles d'Alsace (DNA), Strasbourg's local newspaper, who wanted the bird to combine time-keeping with sound effects.

During the German occupation in the Second World War, the rooster presented a political problem. Seen as too representative of France, it was dismantled and hidden to prevent its destruction. It wasn't until 1944, after the liberation of Strasbourg, that the rooster was reinstalled and regained its voice. Since then, it has crowed daily at noon, marking not just the time but also Strasbourg's enduring resilience.

The building itself has witnessed centuries of history, serving a variety of functions: it was once the residence of Marshal Léonor Marie du Maine du Bourg, governor of Alsace in the 17th century, then a revolutionary tribunal, later a police station, and today, the Hôtel Léonor. And throughout all these changes, the rooster continues to crow proudly from its perch, just as it was intended to when first mounted on the wall.

CLOISTER OF SAINT-PIERRE-LE-JEUNE PROTESTANT CHURCH

7

A little gem often ignored in the heart of the city

Église Saint-Pierre-le-Jeune
Place Saint-Pierre-le-Jeune
Daily 12pm–6pm
Tram C – Broglie stop

Curiously, and despite the notice boards on the left side of the nave, many visitors to the beautiful Saint-Pierre-le-Jeune Protestant church fail to explore its magnificent cloister.

Built in 1050 and restored by Carl Schäfer in the late 19th century, it is not only the oldest cloister north of the Alps, but also one of the rare medieval cloisters preserved in Alsace. Its Romanesque galleries, partly destroyed in the 18th century, were later rebuilt in various styles: one in Gothic, the others in Baroque.

Organised around a square garden planted with trees and flower beds, the cloister's décor is further enriched by murals repainted around the year 2000.

The cloister once belonged to the Chapter of Saint-Pierre-le-Jeune, a community of regular priests who used it for prayer and reflection. Several funerary slabs on the ground recall that it also served as their burial place.

The church itself was divided between Catholics and Protestants after the Reformation, before becoming fully Protestant in 1893.

THE WELL ON PLACE SAINT-PIERRE-LE-JEUNE

⑧

A little-known medieval well

Place Saint-Pierre-le-Jeun (in front of the church)

Many passers-by in Place Saint-Pierre-le-Jeune overlook the small historic well located just a few metres from a luxury hotel.

During the Middle Ages, Strasbourg was supplied with water through a system of public and private wells. The city rests atop one of Europe's most important water tables, with an estimated reserve of 35 billion cubic metres. This abundance made it easy for early inhabitants to access water, as the water table sat only 4 to 8 metres below the surface.

By the late 15th century, Strasbourg was equipped with a wide network of public wells that served nearly every street. By 1704, the city counted 136 wells, and by 1766, the number had grown to 150 — with each well meeting the needs of approximately 200 residents. From the 16th century onward, maintenance was overseen by a designated official, the 'great master of the wells,' and each well was cleaned twice yearly by municipal well-diggers.

Some of these medieval installations are still visible today, including the one in front of Saint-Pierre-le-Jeune church. This sandstone structure features a Renaissance-era rim and is topped with a relief from the late 15th century, depicting Saint Peter and his emblem, the key.

From the 13th century onwards, one of the functions of the town doctor was to advise the magistrate by checking the water supply and ensuring the cleanliness of the town.

The legend of the Cathedral's underground lake

The Notre-Dame de Strasbourg Cathedral (see p. 125 to 163) is steeped in myth and mystery – one of the most enduring being that of an underground lake.

While it is well known that the cathedral was constructed on unstable ground and had to be built on stilts due to the rising water table, local legend adds a supernatural twist: beneath the church lies a shadowy lake, where a ferryman rows silently, transporting the souls of the dead to the afterlife.

In 1681, a soldier in Louis XIV's army is said to have descended into this subterranean world through a cellar in a house still standing on the square. Others reportedly followed. None ever returned.

BAS-RELIEF OF A *MÉSANGE*

⑨

Mésange (Meiselocker, Meise), the nickname of the people of Strasbourg

18, rue de la Mésange

At no. 18, rue de la Mésange, a bas-relief of a *mésange* (tit) feeding on berries pays tribute to a bird that long symbolised Strasbourg's quirky spirit.

The house with the bas-relief decoration named after the mésange (tomtit, chickadee) dates back to 1376.

In the towns and villages of Alsace, the strong personality of local communities is often expressed by humorous nicknames. The Strasbourgeois have long been known as *Meiselocker* or *Meise*, meaning bird-catcher, tit-charmer.

The reason is said to be that each spring young people used to set traps to catch the birds and tame them.

Reed pipes were played to teach them new songs before selling them at the city markets.

This practice continued until the late 19th century, when it was finally banned.

The nickname also extended to the city's artillerymen, whose cannons were compared to bird whistles. In 1552, the people of Strasbourg fired a cannon named Meis at King Henry II, forcing his retreat from Hausbergen.

An impertinent child exchanged for bare buttocks

Strasbourg's attachment to the tomtit was also behind a strange exchange. In 1929 a Meiselocker statue – a cheeky boy charming birds, now on the fountain in Place Saint-Étienne – was imported from Munich.

In exchange Strasbourg sent *Vaterrhine*, representing the Rhine as a male figure. This statue had originally stood in Place Broglie, scandalising opera-going ladies by obligingly presenting its bare buttocks to them.

At the base of the Meiselocker statue is a dialect poem by J.G.D. Arnold (1780), founder of Alsatian dialect theatre. It ends :

JUHE ! IHR BUEWE D'R MORJE-N-ISCH SCHEEN.
DUEN M'R DENN HIT NITT UFF'S MEISELOCKE GEHN ?
DRÜSSE-N-IM RHINWÄLDEL
ODER IM LERCHEFELDEL
GIBT'S ZISELE, BLÖJELE, BRANDLE GENUE.
WER NIE KENN MEISE LOCKT, ISCH AU KENN BUE.

'Hey, you boys, the morning is nice shouldn't we go tit-charming today ? Out in the Rhine forest or in the Lark field there are plenty of birds. If you have never charmed a tit, you are not a real boy.'

Another nickname

The people of Strasbourg are also known as *Steckelburjer*, derived from *Strussburjer* (Strasbourgeois) and *Steckel*, meaning a walking stick. The term originally referred to the bourgeois conversing on benches in Place Kléber.

SCULPTURE OF A LANSQUENET ON RUE DES HALLEBARDES ⑩

An old advertisement for a gunsmith

7, rue des Hallebardes
Tram A, D – Grand'Rue stop

At 7, rue des Hallebardes, on the first floor of a beautiful artisanal house built in 1753 for the widow of goldsmith Jean Daniel Baehr, a discreet but striking stone sculpture catches the eye. It depicts a soldier in traditional dress, holding a halberd — the symbolic weapon of the Lansquenets, those German mercenary foot soldiers who played a key role in European military history in the 15th and 16th centuries. The halberd, combining spear, axe and hook, was prized for its versatility: effective in close combat and capable of dragging mounted knights to the ground.

The gunsmith who once kept shop here used this splendid sculpture as an advertisement, showing the glorious warrior you could become if you bought a weapon from him.

Rue des Hallebardes, named after the Lansquenet's signature weapon, is now lined with halberd motifs along its length, a reminder of Strasbourg's martial past.

Classified in 1927, the three-storey façade is adorned with four mascarons representing the four seasons. The Lansquenet figure, once polychrome, predates the construction of the current façade.

The word *hallebarde* comes from the German *Helmbarte* (*Helm* meaning 'handle', *Barte* meaning 'axe') – a fitting name for this hybrid between spear and axe.

Other Lansquenets in Strasbourg

Two more representations of Lansquenets can be seen in Strasbourg: at 4, quai de la Bruche (see p. 46) and 7, rue du Faubourg National (see p. 42).

For further information about Lansquenets, see p. 43.

DISPLACED ORIEL ON RUE DES HALLEBARDES

11

A little-known reminder of the bombardments of 1944

2, rue des Hallebardes

At the start of Rue des Hallebardes, many overlook a fascinating detail on the façade of the Crédit Mutuel building. A commemorative plaque marks the history of the oriel window installed here – a silent witness to wartime destruction.

Strasbourg, seen as a symbol of Nazi prestige, was bombed three times by the Allies: 6 September 1943, 11 August 1944, 25 September 1944 (see p. 83).

During the second bombing, a 1609 oriel at 3, rue du Fossé des Tailleurs was nearly destroyed.

Fortunately, its elements were rescued by volunteers and, ten years later, reassembled on this current site, where the oriel still stands today.

What is an oriel ?

Reminiscent of the Oriental mashrabiyya and likely derived from medieval bartizans, the oriel is a corbelled window projecting from the façade of a building, often spanning one or more storeys. Though commonly associated with Strasbourg and Alsace, oriels are found throughout France, where they served as symbols of bourgeois affluence.

Beyond their decorative role, oriels had practical advantages: They brought additional light into upper floors, they allowed the wives of wealthy households, who typically stayed indoors, to observe life on the street without being seen and importantly, at a time when building taxes were based on ground-level footprint, oriels offered a way to expand living space without incurring extra tax.

The word oriel comes from Old French *oriol* (porch), through Anglo-Norman *oriell*, and ultimately from Latin *oriollum* – meaning gallery or covered walkway. The English term 'oriel window' retains this original meaning today.

INSCRIPTION 'BNVMGH – IHKEWK' ON RUE DES HALLEBARDES ⑫

A very discreet allusion to a spiritual message

5, rue des Hallebardes
Tram A, D – Grand'Rue stop

At 5, rue des Hallebardes, the oriel on the first floor of the building bears, beneath the windows of its central section, a curious and very discreet inscription composed of twelve initials: *BNVMGH – IHKEWK.*

These initials stand for two German phrases: *Bau Nur Vest Mit Gottes Hand* (Built with the help of the Lord) and *Im Haus Kein Elend Werden Kannt* (The house will not suffer any misfortune).

Built in 1654 by influential bourgeois Jean-Jacques Erhard, this house recalls a time when architecture was still closely linked to expressing divine greatness through form and design. The lines of the oriel are both structured and flowing, in pursuit of a perfect symmetry that echoes the divine order. Its imperial roof evokes the idea of spiritual elevation – a symbolic path to God.

Jean-Jacques Erhard, a member of the Chambers of the XV and XIII (two municipal councils that exercised the city's essential powers – the Council of the XIII for military and foreign affairs, and the Council of the XV for internal affairs), used this inscription to bless his work and ensure its endurance.

The phrase reflects his conviction that the building was constructed under God's guidance, invoking divine blessing to guarantee its solidity, protection from calamities, and the spiritual stability of its occupants.

Although the building was almost entirely destroyed during the bombing of 1944, the oriel and its inscription survived – perhaps proof of the spiritual message's effectiveness in ensuring divine protection?

REPRESENTATION OF MERCURY

(13)

A fragment of an ancient relief on the facade of a restaurant

Façade of the restaurant Chez Yvonne
Between nos. 10 and 12, rue du Sanglier

High up, to the left of the famous restaurant Chez Yvonne on Rue du Sanglier, a fragment of a carved relief can still be seen – part of an ancient votive stele.

It depicts the god Mercury: although his left side is missing, he is recognisable by his face, the caduceus in his hand, and the toga he wears.

This stele is a reminder that other comparable fragments have been discovered in Rue des Frères. According to specialists, a place of worship dedicated to Mercury once existed in the present-day Cathedral district during the Gallo-Roman period.

Among all Gallo-Roman deities, Mercury is the most widely represented in Alsace. As Julius Caesar noted in 'The Gallic Wars', 'They worship Mercury in particular, and have many images of him, and regard him as the inventor of all arts, the guide of their journeys and marches, with great influence over the acquisition of grain and mercantile transactions.'

In Alsace, Mercury is typically shown standing – either naked or draped in a cloak (a *chlamys*) fastened at the shoulder with a fibula. He usually wears a broad-brimmed helmet (the winged petasus), and holds the caduceus in his right hand and a full purse in his left. He is sometimes accompanied by a rooster or a goat; less frequently, he is shown holding a gavel.

This enthusiasm for Mercury stemmed from the fusion of Roman and Gallic religious traditions. As the god of commerce, finance, craftsmanship and trade, Mercury – equivalent to the Greek Hermes – had widespread appeal. He was also considered the messenger of the gods, as well as a patron of war and divination.

His attributes combined those of multiple Celtic and Gallic deities, including Toutatis and Vosegus. Over time, his symbols were adopted as emblems of various professions.

Mercury's caduceus, for example, consists of a laurel or olive branch topped with two wings and entwined by two serpents. Today, this emblem appears on the platform of the French National Assembly, representing trade and eloquence.

It is often confused with the rod of Asclepius, the Roman god of medicine. However, Asclepius' symbol, which became the modern medical emblem, features only one serpent entwined around a staff – without wings.

BAS-RELIEF OF A BOAR

14

A boar lost in translation

15, rue du sanglier
Tram A, D – Grand'Rue stop

For centuries, Rue du Sanglier (Boar Street) has preserved a discreet yet invaluable trace of its past: a bas-relief depicting a wild boar on the façade of No. 15.

Although clearly visible, the sculpture remains little known, hidden by its modest dimensions and tucked-away location.

The street's name itself is the result of a mistranslation. In the 13th century it was called *Hauwartgasse*, after an episcopal official, Mr Hauwart, who supervised the hay stored there. Over time, the name was altered to *Hauergasse*, which in German can mean 'alley (*Gasse*) of the wild boar's defence'. This confusion ultimately gave rise to the present-day name.

The original bas-relief, carved in 1601, measured 72 cm wide by 38.5 cm high. It was destroyed during the bombings of 1944. A faithful reproduction, based on old photographs, was installed here in 1971.

Carved in profile, the boar is shown with a finely chiselled coat, while its slightly forward-facing head reveals imposing tusks – symbols of strength and resilience. The animal appears frozen mid-leap, radiating vigour and determination. This imagery recalls the symbolic power of the wild boar in medieval and Renaissance culture: an emblem of courage and rootedness.

The boar's counterpart, a pendant carving of a wild sow, is preserved at the Musée de l'Œuvre Notre-Dame (see photo).

THE PHALLUS IN THE MAISON KAMMERZELL

15

An artist's prank

Maison Kammerzell
16, place de la cathédrale
03 88 32 42 14

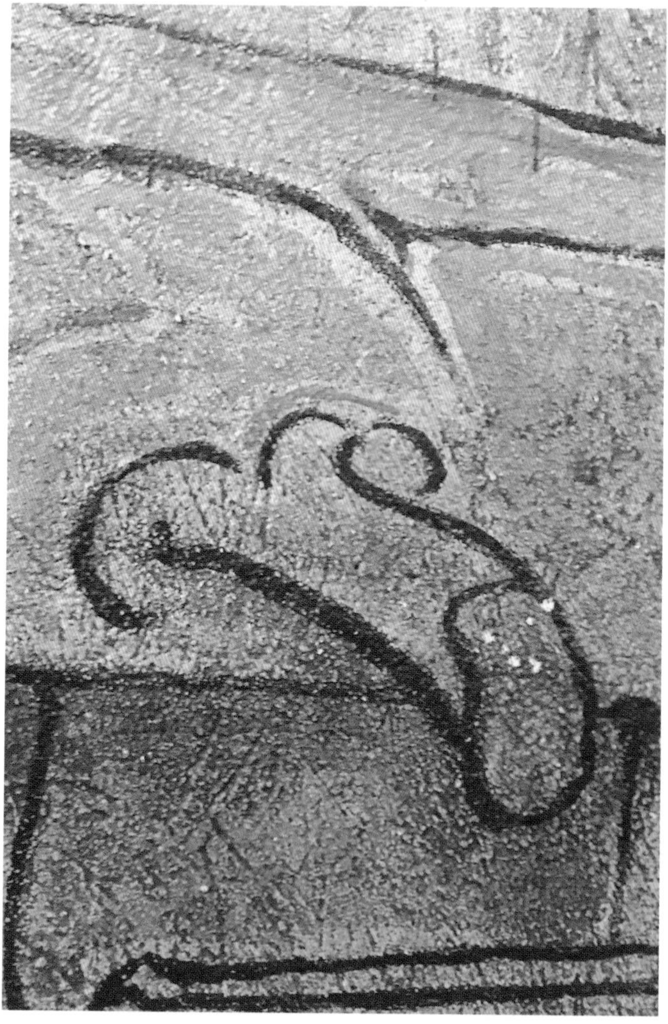

The frescoes adorning the ground floor and first floor of the famous Maison Kammerzell (see below) were created in 1904 by the Strasbourg artist Léo Schnug (1878–1933). Renowned for his passion for 16th-century Rhine painters and his fascination with medieval times, Schnug was even recruited by Emperor Wilhelm II in 1912 to decorate Haut-Koenigsbourg Castle.

Yet Schnug, notorious for his anti-conformist streak and love of alcohol, also enjoyed slipping playful details into his work. On the left wall of a niche on the first floor of the Kammerzell, he painted a male sexual organ – a bawdy detail that often escapes the notice of visitors.

Schnug's imagination was complex: the Middle Ages, madness, anxiety, alcoholism and death were recurring themes in his art. Although the Kammerzell frescoes mostly feature bucolic and allegorical scenes, Schnug wasn't above desecrating the setting with this humorous, irreverent addition.

By 1918, with his health declining, Schnug voluntarily sought treatment for his alcoholism (a condition that had also afflicted his father). After the emotional blow of his mother's death in 1921, he was permanently institutionalised and died in 1933 at the Stephansfeld psychiatric hospital in Brumath.

The Maison Kammerzell

Named after its last private owner, the grocer Philippe-François Kammerzell (who acquired it in 1806), the building was purchased by the Fondation de l'Œuvre Notre-Dame in 1879. By 1895, it had become a popular liquor store. Listed as a historic monument in 1929, it now houses a restaurant.

The Maison Kammerzell has a stone ground floor dating from 1464 and wooden floors added around 1585. These dates are still visible on the façade: the first above a lintel, the second in a panel on the first floor.

Together with the cathedral and the houses on Impasse de la Bière (see p. 188), the Kammerzell is one of the oldest buildings in Strasbourg.

BAS-RELIEF OF VULCAN

⑯

An image of the god of blacksmiths and fire in tribute to metalworkers

25, place de la cathédrale
Tram A, D – Grand'Rue stop

At 25 Place de la Cathédrale, a silent face carved from pink Vosges sandstone gazes out from above a bull's-eye window, overlooking a modest doorway. The face is framed by a set of pliers and a hammer.

The left-hand side of this building was constructed in 1766 for the blacksmith François Saus (the construction date can still be seen engraved in the right bay of the ground floor). The sculpted face is thought to represent Vulcan (or Hephaestus in Greek mythology), the god of blacksmiths and fire – a fitting reference to the forge.

In Roman mythology, Vulcan lived beneath Mount Etna, the famous Sicilian volcano, or on the Aeolian Islands, where he forged streaks of lightning for his father Jupiter (Zeus) and other weapons for the gods.

For Neoplatonist philosophers such as Porphyry of Tyre, Vulcan represented divine fire brought down to Earth. He is often depicted as lame – a consequence, according to myth, of his fall from heaven to the earthly realm. Yet many artists chose to omit this feature, portraying him instead with a hammer in his right hand and pliers in his left.

SECRET LITTLE DRAGON AT THE CATHEDRAL

17

A modern artwork to protect the cornerstone

Strasbourg Cathedral
Tram A, D – Porte-de-l'Hôpital stop – Grand'Rue stop

On the west façade of the cathedral, just a few centimetres above the ground and discreetly tucked into a corner wall, a small metal sculpture may catch the eye of the most attentive passers-by.

Barely larger than a fist, the bronze head of a hybrid creature – half-dragon, half-gargoyle – wears a grumpy expression. Its frowning brow, hooked beak, pointed ears and tiny wings reinforce its fantastical appearance.

Despite its medieval look, this little head is in fact a contemporary addition, installed for a very practical purpose: to protect the cathedral's cornerstone from accidental knocks.

The choice of an animal form is deliberate: it allows this modern feature to blend seamlessly into the cathedral's universe of chimeras, dragons and gargoyles. In doing so, a functional object is transformed into a discreet work of art.

CATHEDRAL ALTIMETER (18)

Discreet memory of the scientific impact of the Prussian Empire

Left wall of the central portal of western façade
Strasbourg Cathedral
Tram A, D – Grand'Rue stop

On the western façade of Strasbourg cathedral, to the left of the central portal, a small cast-iron disc – weather-resistant and firmly anchored into the stone – rarely attracts attention.

Placed about 1.5 metres above the ground, it bears the inscription *Nivellements – Höhenmarke / Meter über Normal Null* ('levelling benchmark / metres above normal zero'), with the figure 144,665.

This figure indicates the altitude, in metres, of the point where it is fixed, according to the German mean height reference system of the time.

Installed in 1882, during the German administration, it was part of the Prussian levelling system based on the *Normalnull* (NN), the altimetric reference then used throughout the Empire.

Following the annexation of Alsace in 1871, the Prussian Empire sought to standardise infrastructure. In 1879, geodesist General Otto von Morozowicz launched a network of altimetric benchmarks based on the average level of the North Sea recorded in Amsterdam. In this context, the Strasbourg Cathedral disc was installed by the Institut Royal de Géodésie du Pays de Bade.

Such benchmarks were used to create precise maps and guide major development projects. By linking reference points, engineers and surveyors could align roads, bridges and water networks with great accuracy.

France uses a different reference system: the Nivellement Général de la France (NGF, General Levelling of France), based on the sea level in Marseille, which produces slight differences in altitude.

FUNERARY MONUMENT OF BISHOP CONRAD OF BUSSNANG ⑲

A little-known work by the famous sculptor Nikolaus von Leyden

Funerary monument of Bishop Conrad of Bussnang Notre-Dame Cathedral
Place de la Cathédrale
Daily, 7am–11.20am and 12.40pm–7pm

Overshadowed by the grandeur of its surroundings, the funerary monument of Bishop Conrad IV of Bussnang (or Bußlingen), who died on 12 March 1471 in Rufach, is often overlooked. His epitaph lies in the chapel of Saint-Jean-Baptiste, to the left of the apse beyond the northern transept.

In the Middle Ages, this chapel served as a burial site for bishops and canons. Conrad's tomb, crafted in 1464, reflects the dimensions reserved for bishops, though he held the episcopal office for only a short time (1439–1440). The original effigy, a recumbent figure, was destroyed in 1686.

The surviving monument features three figures: the bishop, the Virgin Mary, and the infant Jesus.

The interplay between the sacred and the human is striking – Jesus pulls playfully at his mother's veil while placing his hand between those of the praying bishop. The child's mischievous smile lends the piece a rare emotional warmth.

Nikolaus von Leyden

Nikolaus Gerhaert von Leyden (or Nicolaus Gerhaert van Leyden), believed to have been born around 1420–30 in Leiden (modern-day Netherlands), and who died in 1473 in Wiener Neustadt, Austria, is now regarded as one of the most significant northern European sculptors of the late Middle Ages.

Little is known about his life or training. His first signed work dates to 1462 in Trier.

In 1463, he is said to have supervised the construction of the monumental entrance to Strasbourg's Chancellery (now lost).

In 1464, he sculpted the epitaph for Canon Conrad of Bussnang in the Cathedral and was granted bourgeois status in Strasbourg.

THE BREASTFEEDING MERMAID IN THE CATHEDRAL

⑳

A symbol of access to divine knowledge?

Notre-Dame Cathedral
Place de la Cathédrale
Northern crosspiece of the transept
Daily, 7am–11.20am and 12.40pm–7pm

On either side of the baptistery of Notre-Dame Cathedral, two friezes in bas-relief often go unnoticed by visitors. They nevertheless contain representations of fabulous animals in the Romanesque style, dating from around 1190. Among them, one can distinguish the astonishing figure of a mermaid breastfeeding her child.

Mermaids appeared in Christian art as early as the 7th century, as symbols of voluptuousness. Examples can be found in the cathedrals of Basel, Fribourg and Saint-Dié-des-Vosges. Equipped with a caudal fin, these legendary creatures – half woman, half fish – were always depicted with long hair. The nursing mermaid in the Cathedral might symbolise access to divine knowledge: through her breast, evoking spiritual nourishment, she represents the benefits that await the newborns who will be baptised.

The triple immersion of the baptised: secular death to be born to the spiritual life

Water, which remains the essential element of baptisms today, played an even more prominent role in the Middle Ages. In accordance with the practices of antiquity, the ritual was performed through complete immersion. Since the babies were submerged three times in succession, they would stop breathing, evoking a symbolic phase of death. When they emerged from the water of the baptistery, they were brought back into the world of the living: symbolically, they left the secular life to be born into the spiritual life.

These 'three times' echoed the Christian Trinity. Over the centuries, the practice of immersion was gradually replaced by simple sprinkling.

A surprising seven-sided baptistery

Sculpted by Master Jodoque Dotzinger in 1453, the baptismal font of Notre-Dame Cathedral is heptagonal (seven-sided).

This is unusual, as baptisteries were generally designed with eight sides – eight being the symbolic number for baptism and resurrection. According to Christian tradition, God created the world in six days and rested on the seventh.

The eighth day symbolises the resurrection of Jesus. Baptism, which marks entry into the Catholic Church and faith in Christ's message of hope, is thus associated with this number: through baptism, humankind embarks on the path to eternal life.

SCULPTURE OF ST ALEXIUS

㉑

Artwork hidden under the stairs

Under the staircase of the cathedral pulpit
Monday to Saturday 8.30am–11.15am & 12.45–5.45pm
Sunday and public holidays 2pm–5.15pm
Tram A, D – Grand'Rue stop

The sculpture depicting the legend of St Alexius is a remarkable Gothic work discreetly placed within Strasbourg Cathedral, one of Alsace's most emblematic monuments. This masterpiece, created by Hans Hammer in 1485, is easy to miss because of its position beneath the staircase leading to the pulpit.

The 15th-century statue portrays an episode from the life of St Alexius, a symbol of humility and renunciation (see following double-page spread).

The saint is shown sitting under a staircase, one hand supporting his face, the other holding a note recounting his life. The scene recalls how he lived for 17 years beneath the stairs in his parents' home, unrecognised by them and mistaken for a beggar.

The ensemble is in the late Gothic style, distinguished by elegant, expressive forms. It displays the naturalistic attention to detail characteristic of sculptors of the late Middle Ages, particularly in the folds of the saint's garments and the expressions of the surrounding figures.

There is also a striking additional detail: above St Alexius, a character appears to be tipping something over his head – probably a servant throwing out the rubbish.

For more on the extraordinary life of St Alexius, see following double-page spread.

The extraordinary life of St Alexius, who slept for 17 years under the stairs

According to legend, Alexius was miraculously born in Rome to noble parents who had long been unable to have children. The son of Senator Euphemian and his wife, Algas, he grew up in the lap of luxury during the reign of the emperors Honorius (395–423) and Arcadius (395–408). Against his will, he was betrothed to a virtuous young girl, but on the eve of their wedding Alexius persuaded her to renounce marriage. That same day he fled to Odessa (present-day Turkey), where he embraced the life of an ascetic. Having sold all his possessions to aid the poor, he lived as a beggar in the porch of the Church of the mother of God (Theotokos), imposing upon himself a life of extreme mortification. When the church porter discovered his identity and revealed his holiness, crowds began to gather. Out of humility, Alexius left Odessa and sailed for Tarsus in Cilicia (present-day Turkey), the homeland of St Paul. But contrary winds – or perhaps fate – carried him instead to Ostia, the port of Rome. From there he returned to his father's house. Although his fiancée had remained faithful, neither she nor his parents recognised him. His miserable clothing, wasted body and altered features disguised him completely. Believing him to be a beggar, his family allowed him to stay beneath the outside steps of their house. Alexius lived there, unnoticed, for 17 years. Every day his former servants insulted him and threw rubbish at him, though his father ordered that he be given food out of pity. As death approached, Alexius wrote the story of his life on a roll of paper. When he died, a heavenly voice revealed his presence to the emperor and the pope. Looking beneath the steps, they found his body, still clutching the scroll that recounted his origins.

A saint no longer Catholic

Celebrated on 17 February by the Orthodox Church, St Alexius was also celebrated by the Roman Catholic Church on 17 July until 1969, when the Second Vatican Council (1962–65) classified him among the 'saints who present serious historical difficulties', as his very existence had long been in doubt. He was therefore officially removed from the list of saints whose worship is authorised by the Catholic Church.

Part of the original staircase is preserved in Rome, at the Basilica dei Santi Bonifacio e Alessio (Saint Boniface and Saint Alexius), in the Testaccio district. See 'Secret Rome', also published by Jonglez.

FORGOTTEN FESTIVALS OF THE PERPETUAL CALENDAR OF THE ASTRONOMICAL CLOCK

22

Who today remembers the Feast of Quasimodo, which inspired Victor Hugo's Quasimodo?

Astronomical clock
Strasbourg Cathedral
Monday to Saturday 8.30am–11.15am and 12.45pm–5.45pm
Sunday and public holidays 2pm–5.15pm
Tram A, D – Porte-de-l'Hôpital stop – Grand'Rue stop

At the heart of Strasbourg Cathedral, the famous astronomical clock discreetly records in gold letters, at the top of its perpetual calendar, a number of festivals that have fallen into oblivion: the Feast of the Four Seasons, the Feast of Saint Arbogast, the Septuagesima, the Feast of Quasimodo...

Observed four times a year, the Feast of the Four Seasons was a period of fasting, prayer and penance, established to thank God for the fruits of nature and sanctify the cycle of the seasons. Dating back to early Christianity and formalised by Pope Gregory I (540–604), these days were also linked to priestly ordinations and spiritual renewal.

They fell on three consecutive days – Wednesday, Friday and Saturday – after Ash Wednesday (spring), after Pentecost (summer), around 14 September (Feast of the Holy Cross, autumn), and after Saint Lucia's Day, 13 December (winter).

Strictly observed with rigor for centuries, the Four Seasons gradually disappeared from practice after the Second Vatican Council (1962–1965), although some communities still celebrate them. On the Strasbourg clock, this festival is therefore mentioned four times, once per season.

Celebrated on 21 July, Saint Arbogast was once one of the most revered figures in Alsatian Christianity, though his memory is now largely forgotten outside Strasbourg.

Arbogast, who may have been originally from Aquitaine, Franconia, or even Ireland according to tradition, became Bishop of Strasbourg in the 7th century.

A man of asceticism and prayer who lived in seclusion in the forests of Alsace, he was called upon to become pastor of a region that was still largely pagan. He is credited with works of Christianization, the construction of churches, and even a miracle: the resurrection of King Dagobert's son.

A model of humility and charity, he was buried at Saint-Thomas Church in Strasbourg.

His feast day, although still included in the diocesan calendar, has lost the prominence it once had, despite his remarkable presence on the clock.

Septuagesima Sunday, now almost forgotten, once marked a key stage in the liturgical cycle. It marked the beginning of a period of preparation for Lent, three weeks before Ash Wednesday (a movable feast that marks the beginning of Lent, 47 days before Easter – the day before Ash Wednesday, Mardi Gras, is the last 'fat' day before Lent, which lasts 40 days).

The 'time of Septuagesima' also included Sexagesima (60 days before Easter) and Quinquagesima (50 days).

MARS
6 A Les Cendres
7 B s. Fridolin ab.
8 C s. Thomas d'Aq.
9 D s. Jean de Dieu
10 E sᵗᵉ Françoise
11 F Les 40 Mart.
12 G s. Euloge mart.
13 A Quatre Temps
14 B sᵗᵉ Euphrasie
15 C sᵗᵉ Mathilde im.
16 D s. Zacharie
17 E s. Héribert év.
18 F sᵗᵉ Gertrude
19 G s. Gabriel arc.
20 A s. Joseph
21 B s. Alexandre
22 C s. Bénoit abbé
23 D s. Emile erm.
24 E sᵗᵉ Pélagie pen.
25 F s. Irénée év. m.
26 G Annonciation
27 A s. Ludgar évêq.
28 B s. Rupert évêq.
C s. Gontran
D s. Eustache ab.
E s. Quirinus
F sᵗᵉ Balbina vge
G s. Hugues év.
s. Franç. de P.
s. Richard év.
s. Isidore év. d.
sᵗᵉ Perpétue
La Passion
s. Rodolph év.
Edèse mart.
Marie Cléop.
Hégésippe
VIII
VII

During this time, the faithful already adopted a more austere liturgy, ceasing to sing Hallelujah and preparing for the penance of Lent.

Septuagesima symbolized a call to conversion, a time for reflection on the human condition and the need for salvation.

Suppressed in the reforms of the Second Vatican Council, the feast is still celebrated in the Tridentine Mass and in some Anglican and Orthodox traditions. Its appearance on the clock reminds us of its once central role in preparing for Easter.

Quasimodo Sunday, the first Sunday after Easter, takes its name from the Latin introit *Quasi modo geniti infantes, alleluia* ('As newborn babes, hallelujah'). This day was dedicated in particular to the newly baptized, who on this day returned the white garments they had received during the Easter Vigil. Spiritually, it is a celebration of the renewal of faith.

In 2000, this Sunday was also designated as Divine Mercy Sunday by

Pope John Paul II, in connection with the revelations of Saint Faustina in the 1930s.

This day also inspired the name of the character Quasimodo in Victor Hugo's novel The Hunchback of Notre-Dame: it was on Quasimodo Sunday that the priest Claude Frollo took him in on the cathedral steps and adopted him.

The clock itself is a remarkable work of art, with its intricate mechanism and design. It is a testament to the skill and ingenuity of the craftsmen who created it.

STAINED-GLASS WINDOW OF ONE HUNDRED FACES

23

A spectacular contemporary stained-glass window

Chapel of St Catherine
Strasbourg Cathedral
Monday to Saturday: 8.30am–11.15am & 12.45pm–5.45pm
Sunday and public holidays 2pm–5.15pm

In the heart of the cathedral, tucked away in the Chapel of St Catherine, is a striking contemporary work often overlooked by visitors: the 'stained-glass window of one hundred faces'. Inaugurated in 2015 to mark the cathedral's millennium, it fills two windows that were previously bare.

On the right-hand side, in an enigmatic manner, the face of Christ in blessing (his left hand resting on the windowsill) rises almost the full height of the window (8.7 metres).

Inspired by Hans Memling's 'Christ Giving His Blessing' (1481), preserved at the Museum of Fine Arts in Boston, the face has a distinctive feature: it is composed of over a hundred photographs of Strasbourg residents, from a wide variety of origins, generations, and backgrounds, assembled in mosaic form.

The left-hand window (9 metres high) shows, alongside Christ's right hand raised in blessing, a composite landscape made from photographs of nature.

This evokes the words attributed to St Catherine of Alexandria: 'Contemplate nature, and you will see God there.'

The ensemble is realised through an innovative technique of glass photography, combining digital printing, traditional painting on glass, and lead framing.

The work is the fruit of a collaboration between photographer Véronique Ellena and master glassmaker Pierre-Alain Parot. While rooted in the great tradition of religious stained glass, it offers a strikingly new visual conception.

The mosaic Christ reflects the multiplicity of humanity, overturning the classic iconography: rather than a single idealised face, here Christ embodies a living, contemporary plurality.

The stained glass thus reminds us that the Church is inhabited by the men and women of today, with Christ becoming a mirror of the human community.

FUNERARY STELE OF ERWIN OF STEINBACH

(24)

A master builder whose reputation fascinated Goethe

Notre-Dame Cathedral
To visit this part of the Cathedral, which is usually closed, send a written request: Presbytère de la Cathédrale Notre-Dame de Strasbourg
1, rue de Rohan - BP09 – 67060 Strasbourg Cedex (03 88 21 43 34)

In a small courtyard to the north of the Saint-Jean chapel at Notre-Dame Cathedral (accessible by reservation), a funerary stele recalls the life of Erwin, also known as 'von Steinbach' (1244–1318), a German architect and sculptor.

Though his exact place of birth is debated, Erwin is thought to have come from one of several towns named Steinbach. He is considered the principal master builder of the cathedral, his name appearing in a contract from the Œuvre Notre-Dame dated 16 October 1284, where he is referred to as 'Werkmeister Erwin.' He is credited with completing the monumental gates by around 1290 and assembling the Grande Rose window before 1298.

After his death, he was buried in the cathedral's open courtyard, but the location of his grave was forgotten for centuries. It was rediscovered in 1816, hidden under a pile of coal in the courtyard beside the chapel of Saint-Jean-Baptiste.

The Latin epitaph on his funerary stele, carved in Gothic capital letters, reads: 'On 21 July of the year of Our Lord 1316, died Husa, wife of Master Erwin, On 17 January of the year of Our Lord 1318, died Master Erwin, Gubernator of the Strasbourg Münster factory, on 18 March of the year of Our Lord 1339, died Master John, son of Erwin, the foreman of this church.'

Erwin's other son, Gerlach, became the master builder of the collegiate church of Saint-Florent in Niedcrhaslach from 1295. He died accidentally in 1330 and was buried there.

Goethe's concept of genius

In November 1772, the young Goethe (1749–1832) dedicated his essay 'Von deutscher Baukunst' (On German Architecture) to Master Erwin. In this text, emblematic of the Sturm und Drang movement, Goethe, who had discovered the cathedral in 1770, develops his conception of genius and true art based on what he felt during his visit. A genius does not create his works from ready-made ideas, but from his own creative force – like the master Erwin von Steinbach. Curiously, Goethe cites the architecture of Italy and even France – the country that gave rise to the Gothic style that so impressed him in Strasbourg – as counter-examples to true art.

GRAFFITI ON THE PLATFORM OF NOTRE-DAME CATHEDRAL

25

Where great authors came to marvel

Place de la cathédrale
1 April–30 September: 9.30am–8pm (last climb at 7.30pm)
1 October–31 March: 10am–6pm (last climb at 5.30pm)
Closed : 1 January, 1 May, 25 December
Paid entry (free on first Sundays of the month and European Heritage Days)

To reach the platform of Notre-Dame Cathedral, perched 66 metres high, visitors must climb 330 steps of a spiralling staircase. The effort is rewarded by stunning panoramic views through openings along the way.

In the 18th and 19th centuries, the platform served as à social space. Acrobats performed, drinks were served, and games were played. Telescopes allowed curious onlookers to scan the horizon.

For a small fee, visitors could even have their names engraved into the stone - and many did. One of the most famous signatures is that of Johann Wolfgang von Goethe (1749–1832), still visible at the foot of the high tower's octagon.

In 1770 Goethe spent an academic year in Strasbourg where he studied law, chemistry and anatomy.

On his arrival he was deeply moved by the cathedral – a real emotional experience for him. He got into the habit of visiting the platform at the time 'when young classmates meet there towards evening, to greet the sunset with glass in hand', as he wrote.

Goethe appreciated his stay in Strasbourg so much that he once said: 'I'm beginning to really like case law. It's just like Strasbourg beer; the first time it repels you, and when you've drunk it for a week you can no longer do without it.'

Victor Hugo's 'perpendicular journey'

Victor Hugo visited Strasbourg in 1839 and climbed to the platform, describing the experience in En Voyage (Volume I, letters XXIX–XXX) :

'All of a sudden, at a fork in the road, the mist lifted and I saw the Münster. It was six o'clock in the morning.

The enormous cathedral, the highest summit built by the hand of man after the Great Pyramid, stood against a backdrop of magnificently-shaped dark mountains, with large valleys intermittently bathed in sunlight.

The work of God made for men, the work of men made for God, the mountain and the cathedral competed for greatness. I have never seen anything more imposing...

Having seen the church, I climbed the bell tower. You know my taste for perpendicular journeys. I wouldn't have missed the tallest spire in the world.'

THE LITTLE DOG IN THE CATHEDRAL

(26)

An animal that roused the somnolent faithful

Notre-Dame Cathedral
Third northern column of the nave

On the eastern side of the staircase of the pulpit in Notre-Dame Cathedral – built in 1485 for the preacher and moralist Johann Geiler von Kaysersberg (1445–1510) – you can spot the figure of a small dog.

Johann Geiler, invited to preach at the cathedral, remained in Strasbourg from 1478 until his death. At the time, the city's authorities were determined to restore the cathedral's dignity, as it had lost its sacred status. Vagabonds camped inside at night, while residents of Strasbourg used it as a shortcut by day. Some even walked through with their animals, especially pigs. Since place de la Cathédrale was not yet paved, the floor became covered in mud and excrement. People also sought shelter from the rain, prostituted themselves or traded goods inside, showing no respect for the sacred nature of the monument (see p. 169).

Geiler preached there on Sundays, holidays and every day during Lent. His sermons were famous not only for their biblical references but also for vivid depictions of the vices of his time, which made a lasting impression on listeners. And if anyone happened to fall asleep during his preaching, his little dog would bark to wake them up! Geiler owned a Bichon Frise – a fashionable breed in the 15th century.

Since then, the depiction of this little dog has been thought to bring good luck to those who stroke it: its head has darkened over time due to the countless hands that have sought its blessing.

Dogs often appear at the feet of recumbent statues on medieval tombs, representing loyalty – Christians' faithfulness to God.

SKELETON UNDER THE CRUCIFIXION CROSS

27

Link between Adam, his body, his skull, Golgotha and Jesus ...

Tympanum of the cathedral's central portal
Tram A, D – Porte de l'Hôpital stop – Grand'Rue stop

Among the countless sculptural wonders of the cathedral, a remarkable detail on the tympanum of the central portal often goes unnoticed. Beneath the scene of the crucifixion, an entire skeleton lies at the feet of Christ – a rare and striking representation.

This is Adam, the first man of the Bible, accompanied by Eve, both carved in relief.

The hill of the crucifixion was called Golgotha in Aramaic, the language of Jesus – a word meaning 'skull'. According to tradition, this was also the place where Adam's body was buried. His skull was revealed at the time of Christ's crucifixion, giving the site its name.

Christian tradition teaches that the sacrifice and resurrection of Christ erase original sin, for which Adam was responsible, thus offering salvation to all humankind.

Adam is depicted lying down, almost like a body in a tomb. His skeleton is rendered with precision: prominent ribs, a clearly defined skull. The Cross seems to spring directly from his body, underlining the link between the Fall and Redemption.

In Christian iconography, only a skull is usually shown at the foot of the Cross. Here, however, the sculptor chose to depict the entire body, intensifying the message: Christ redeems not just the soul, but the whole of humanity, body and spirit alike.

For 13th-century theology, this recalled the importance of the resurrection of the flesh – death being not an end, but a passage towards eternal life.

THE GLASS SLOT IN THE MERIDIAN BY JEAN-BAPTISTE SCHWILGUÉ

28

A vestige of time measurement

Strasbourg Cathedral - South portal and transept
Monday to Saturday, 8.30am–11.15am and 12.45pm–5.45pm; Sunday, 2pm–5.15pm
Free admission
Trams A and D - Porte de l'Hôpital stop - Grand'Rue stop

Few Strasbourg residents, let alone tourists, notice a discreet glass slit in the upper part of the south portal. However, it plays a fundamental role as a gnomon for the sundial installed by J.B. Schwilgué between 1838 and 1843 in Strasbourg Cathedral, to the right of the astronomical clock.

The system works as follows: the glass slit allows a ray of light to pass through which, based on precise calculations of the ray's trajectory according to the latitude and inclination of the building, reaches the sundial (in the form of a vertical graduated ruler) inside the cathedral at the moment of true solar noon.

The light beam is shaped by a tiny folded metal plate located above the glass slit, which goes completely unnoticed.

The Schwilgué meridian is one of many examples of the advances in time measurement techniques in the 19th century. It illustrates the expertise of Schwilgué, who was a clockmaker, mathematician, and engineer. It was used primarily to calibrate and adjust the astronomical clock with great precision (until 1875), to check variations in solar time, and to understand the differences between solar time and mean time. It was primarily used to calibrate and adjust the astronomical clock with great precision (until 1875), to check variations in solar time and to understand the differences between solar time and mean time (which were then corrected by the equation of time). At a time when mechanical clocks were not yet completely reliable, a meridian instrument was still essential for adjusting public clocks. It was also used by astronomers and scientists for their observations.

Remarkable for its scientific precision, it remains a fascinating vestige of the history of time measurement.

For more information about the meridians, see the following double-page spread.

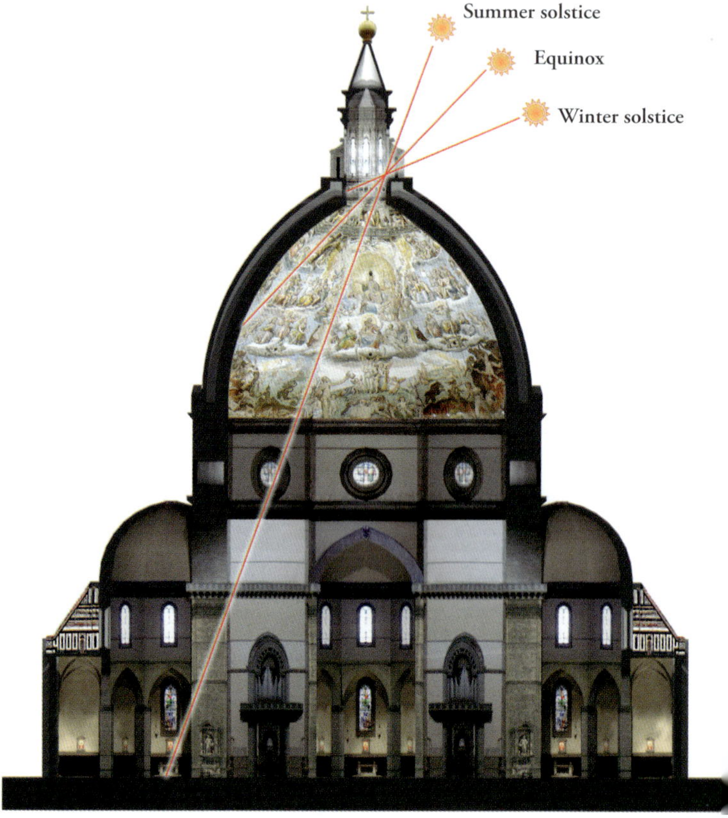
Summer solstice
Equinox
Winter solstice

How does a meridian work?

Instead of the shadow of a gnomon, meridians use a small hole placed at a certain height, through which the sun's light falls onto a meridian line (i.e. one aligned exactly north-south). The fact that the sun's rays perform the function of the shadow in a traditional sundial means that the opening is sometimes referred to as a 'gnomonic opening'. The higher the opening, the more efficient the meridian, hence the interest in using cathedrals (see following double-page spread); the circumference of the hole had to be no more than one thousandth of the height above the ground. Obviously, the opening had to be installed on the south side of the building in order to let in the rays of the sun, which lies to the south in the northern hemisphere.

The meridian line should run from the point which stands perpendicularly below the axis of the opening, not always easy to determine using the instruments available to scientists in the past (see preceding double page). The length of the line depends on the height of the opening; in some cases, where the building was not long enough to trace the entire meridian line across the floor (as was the case at Saint-Sulpice in Paris), an obelisk was added at its end, so that the movement of the sun's rays could then be measured up the vertical. In summer, when the sun is highest in the sky, the rays fall onto the meridian line closer to the south wall (where that line begins) than they do in winter, when the sun is lower over the horizon and the rays tend to strike towards the far end of the meridian line.

The main principle behind the working of the meridian is that at noon, solar time, the sun is at its apex and, by definition, its rays fall straight along a line running exactly north-south. So, the exact moment when those rays strike the meridian line, which does run north-south, indicates solar noon. Furthermore, the exact place on the meridian line where that ray falls makes it possible to determine the day of the year: the point right at the beginning of the line is reached solely on the day of the summer solstice, whilst the exact end of the line is reached on the day of the winter solstice. Experience and observation meant that the meridian line could be calibrated to identify different days of the year.

Once this was done, the line could be used to establish the date of various movable feasts, such as Easter – one of the great scientific and religious uses of meridians. Similarly, the different periods corresponding with the signs of the Zodiac could be established, which explains why such signs are indicated along the length of a number of meridian lines.

Why was October 4 followed immediately by October 15 in the year 1582? The measurement of time and the origin of the meridians

The entire problem of the measurement of time and the establishment of calendars arises from the fact that the Earth does not take an exact number of days to orbit the sun: one orbit in fact takes neither 365 nor 366 days but rather 365 days, 5 hours, 48 minutes and 45 seconds.
At the time of Julius Caesar, Sosigenes of Alexandria calculated this orbit as 365 days and 6 hours. In order to make up for this difference of an extra 6 hours, he came up with the idea of an extra day every four years: thus the Julian calendar – and the leap year – came into being.
In 325 BCE, the Council of Nicacea established the temporal power of the Church (it had been called by Constantine, the first Roman emperor to embrace Christianity). The Church's liturgical year contained fixed feasts such as Christmas, but also movable feasts such as Easter. The latter was of essential importance as it commemorated the death and resurrection of Christ, and so the Church decided that it should fall on the first Sunday following the full moon after the spring equinox. That year, the equinox fell on March 21, which was thus established as its permanent date. However, over the years, observation of the heavens showed that the equinox (which corresponds with a certain known position of the stars) no longer fell on March 21.The 11 minutes and 15 seconds difference between the real and assumed time of the Earth's orbit around the sun was resulting in an increasing gap between the actual equinox and March 21. By the sixteenth century, that gap had increased to ten full days and so Pope Gregory XIII decided to intervene. Quite simply, ten days would be removed from the calendar in 1582, and it would pass directly from October 4 to October 15. It was also decided, on the basis of complex calculations (carried out most notably by the Calabrian astronomer Luigi Giglio), that the first year of each century (ending in 00) would not actually be a leap year, even though divisible by four. The exceptions would fall every 400 years, which would mean that in 400 years there would be a total of just 97 (rather than 100) leap years. This came closest to making up the shortfall resulting from the difference between the real and assumed time of orbit. Thus 1700, 1800 and 1900 would not be leap years, but 2000 would.
In order to establish the full credibility of this new calendar – and convince the various Protestant nations that continued to use the Julian calendar – Rome initiated the installation of large meridians within its churches. A wonderful scientific epic had begun.

The meridian of Santa Maria del Fiore: the highest in the world

From the 15th to the 18th century almost 70 meridians were installed in churches in France and Italy. Only 10, however, have a gnomonic opening that is more than 10 metres above floor level – that height being crucial to the accuracy of the instrument:

S. S. Maria del Fiore (Florence)	90.11 m
S. Petronio (Bologna)	27.07 m
St-Sulpice (Paris)	26.00 m
Monastery of San Nicolo l'Arena (Catania, Sicily)	23.92 m
Cathedral (Milan)	23.82 m
S. Maria degli Angeli (Rome)	20.34 m
Collège de l'Oratoire (Marseille)	17.00 m
S. Giorgio (Modica, Sicily)	14.18 m
Museo Nazionale (Naples)	14.00 m
Cathedral (Palermo)	11.78 m

Why were meridians installed in cathedrals?

To make their measurements more precise, astronomers required enclosed spaces where the point admitting light was as high as possible from the ground: the longer the beam of light, the more accurately they could establish that it was meeting the floor along an exactly perpendicular plane. Cathedrals were soon recognised as the ideal location for such scientific instruments as meridians. Furthermore, the Church had a vested interest, because meridians could be used to establish the exact date of Easter.

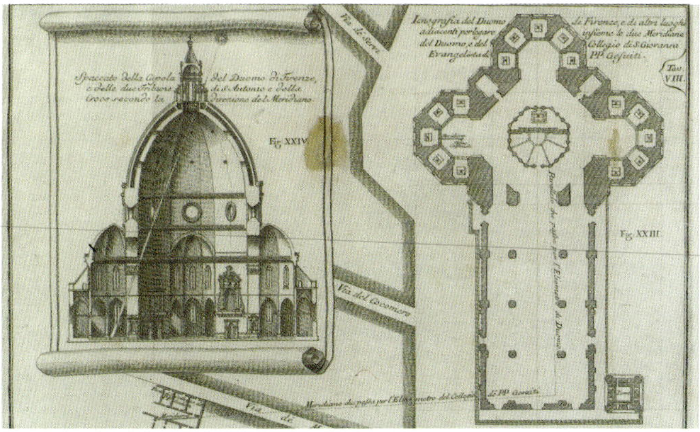

MEASUREMENT OF THE CORBELS

(29)

A medieval inscription, evidence of fire prevention in Strasbourg

Right wall of south door of cathedral
Tram A, D – Porte de l'Hôpital stop – Grand'Rue stop

A discreet inscription to the right of the south door of Strasbourg Cathedral is easily missed.

Engraved directly into the sandstone, in an elongated rectangular frame, the medieval German inscription in sober but legible typography reads: *Dies ist die Masz des Überhanges* ('This is the measurement of the corbels').

The frame serves as a visual reference, marking the maximum permissible width of corbels – a cantilever of 1.08 metres – for the upper floors of half-timbered houses.

This regulation was adopted after the devastating fire of 1298. Caused by an unextinguished lamp in a nearby stable, the blaze destroyed 355 houses, damaged the cathedral roof, and melted its bells.

In response to the disaster, Strasbourg's magistrates implemented several preventive measures: limiting the projection of upper floors, widening streets, constructing a firewall, and enhancing firefighting capacity. The inscription on the cathedral wall served as an official reference, visible to all, guaranteeing compliance with the new regulation.

At a time when living space was precious and taxed, corbelled constructions were used to increase floor area without encroaching on ground space. However, they also posed a serious fire hazard by enabling flames to spread more easily from one building to another. Strict application of the 1.08-metre limit greatly reduced the spread of fires from 1400 onwards.

The effects of this medieval regulation are still visible today: a recent study of around 100 corbelled houses in Strasbourg found that 90% respect the medieval limit, with an average cantilever of 0.75 metres.

TRACES OF FORMER STALLS ON THE CATHEDRAL (30)

The remains of an inglorious past

Notre-Dame Cathedral
Neo-gothic galleries located on the north and south sides of the building
Place de la Cathédrale, before Rue des Frères, and Place du Château

For centuries, Notre-Dame Cathedral was surrounded by dubious activity, with all manner of disreputable characters conducting their often-questionable business both inside and outside the building (see p. 169). From medieval times onwards, stalls and small houses were built in a haphazard fashion along the north and south sides of the cathedral, leaning against its walls and buttresses. Although these constructions have long been demolished, traces remain for the observant eye: black lines along the monument's sides mark the original positions of the shack frames.

Before their demolition, these unsightly constructions were largely hidden from view. Between 1772 and 1778, Jean-Laurent Goetz (1723–1809), architect of the Fondation de l'Œuvre Notre-Dame, replaced them with uniform shopfronts. He also erected large galleries in the Gothic style to further conceal these buildings. Known today as the Goetz galleries, they were among the earliest examples of neo-Gothic architecture in Alsace. The rosettes adorning the spandrels, however, were characteristic of the Louis XVI style.

Goetz also added gargoyles to lend the cathedral a more medieval appearance – very much in vogue from the late 18th century.

In 1848, following a decision by the Council, all the stalls were demolished. The old doors of the galleries that concealed the shops were then replaced by bay windows under the direction of the architect Gustave Klotz (see below), who aimed to transform the galleries into protective fences shielding the cathedral's side walls from the bustle of the city.

Gustave Klotz

Appointed in 1838, Gustave Klotz (1810–1880), architect of the Fondation de l'Œuvre Notre-Dame, served in this role for over 40 years. His most notable work involved restoring the cathedral after the Prussian bombing of 1870 (see p. 206). He also designed the choir vault, known as the 'Klotz Tower,' which was later heavily damaged by Allied bombing in 1944 (see p. 83).

Klotz was also responsible for other significant buildings in Strasbourg, including the Hôtel de la Préfecture, the Palais de Justice, the stud farm, the prisons of the gendarmerie barracks, and the building at no. 5, place du Château.

STORKS ON THE CATHEDRAL FAÇADE

31

The cathedral's first lightning rods

Notre-Dame Cathedral

Among the many carved figures on the façade of Notre-Dame Cathedral, few passers-by notice the storks perched at the north-west and south-west corners. These birds, though often overlooked today, held deep symbolic meaning for the cathedral's original builders.

For centuries, the white stork – now an icon of Strasbourg and Alsace – was seen as a good luck charm and a harbinger of good fortune (see following double-page spread).

The workers of the 11th century believed this too. After a lightning strike destroyed the building in 1007, superstition halted its reconstruction. The builders were reluctant to continue, fearing another divine punishment – until storks began nesting on the scaffolding.

Storks were believed to protect homes from lightning and fire. By the 12th century, they had even become a protected species. In 1015, Bishop Werner I of Habsburg and Emperor Henry II of the Holy Roman Empire laid the foundation stone of a new cathedral atop the ruins.

Despite this folkloric protection, a real lightning rod was not installed until 1835. The idea had first emerged in the late 18th century, driven by the war commissioner Jean Jacques Théodose Le Barbier de Tinan (1738–1791).

A passionate follower of scientific progress, Le Barbier de Tinan translated the letters of Alessandro Volta and a treatise by Giuseppe Toaldo, and wrote 'Mémoire sur la manière d'armer d'un conducteur la cathédrale de Strasbourg in 1780'. He submitted it to the Académie royale des sciences, which approved the project—although implementation was delayed by over 50 years.

The legend of the white stork, a symbol of fertility and fidelity

The first known written version of the white stork legend, connecting the bird to fertility and childbirth, dates back to 1840 in Lower Germany.

The story, also called the 'Legend of the Kindelesbrunnen' or 'Legend of the Children's Wells' in Alsatian, was popularised by a poem that reads: 'Storick, Storick, Stork, Stork, bend your legs Bring a nice kid to mother…' This legend reached wider audiences through the printed imagery of Jean Frédéric Wentzel (1807–1869) in Wissembourg.

In this tale, storks retrieve children from pools or springs, where elves tend to souls fallen with the rain from the sky, transforming them into babies. In Germanic mythology, water is the cradle of souls awaiting reincarnation, and the stork – linked to birth – is the messenger of the goddess Holda.

G. Illberg, in 'Lacs, étangs des Vosges - histoire, légendes' (André Bonne, 1967) recounts a similar version from Strasbourg: 'In the city flows a fountain called the Fischbrunnen. When a mama wants to have a beautiful healthy baby, she goes to this fountain and calls upon the pond's little elf through the waterpipe. Once in touch with him, she tells him to find her a boy or a girl, as he chooses. When the request is made, the elf takes his golden-meshed net and fishes a baby from the depths […]. Boys, being stronger, always surface first.

As soon as a baby is caught in the net and lifted out of the water, the sounds of cathedral organs and chanters are heard. Then a priest begins to recite prayers.

When everything is again quiet in the cathedral, by pressing your ear against the stonework you can hear a boat rowing towards the end of the lake, where the elf gives the chosen baby to a stork standing on one leg.

Taking it in her long beak, she carries it to the eagerly awaiting mother who made the request. Once the stork flies off, the secret gateway to the lake closes.

Anyone nearby at that very moment could supposedly hear this cry from the many babies: '*Komma ni geh hola!*' ('Come and get us!').'

This legend is also a variant of the myth of the cathedral's underground lake, across which a ferryman was said to carry the souls of the dead (see p. 107).

The modern link between storks and baby delivery didn't appear in Alsace until after 1870. August Stoeber (1808–1884) noted that 'storks do not begin to nest until they hear German spoken,' while the illustrator Hansi (Jean-Jacques Waltz, 1873–1951) reinterpreted the symbol as a sign of French resilience.
Today, the white stork remains one of the most beloved emblems of Strasbourg and Alsace.

'CAVEAU POUR LE FUTUR !' (32)

An original reflection on time and memory

Place du Château
Tram A, D – Porte de l'Hôpital stop – Grand'Rue stop

The magnificent monuments around Place du Château attract plenty of passers-by, yet few notice a pioneering work of prospective archaeology embedded in the paving of the square, walked over daily by Strasbourg residents who remain unaware of its presence.

'Caveau pour le futur' (Vault for the Future), created in 1995 by Strasbourg artist Raymond-Emile Waydelich, is covered by a bronze plaque. The installation was part of the exhibition 'Mutarotnegra: 3790 après Jésus-Christ' at the Musée Archéologique.

The inscription reads: 'Here is preserved for the future a part of our memory. To be opened only on 23 September of the year 3790 AD.' This phrase immediately conveys the idea of a time capsule intended for future generations, reflecting the artist's fascination with prospective archaeology.

Beneath the slab lies a gigantic barrel containing objects representative of late 20th-century civilisation. Among them are a Roger Siffer record, condoms symbolising public health, Coca-Cola cans as emblems of global consumer culture, the European Convention on Human Rights, and items contributed by local residents.

This eclectic collection is designed to provide future archaeologists with an authentic view of our era, capturing everyday life at the end of the 20th century.

The installation goes beyond the mere preservation of objects. It is a reflection on time, memory, and the consequences of our present choices. It invites self-examination: what do we choose to pass on, and how will future generations interpret our age?

Waydelich imagines a museum of the present, prompting us to consider how our practices will be studied after our disappearance. By curating specific objects, he draws attention to contemporary social and environmental concerns, urging us to think about the legacy we leave behind and the sustainability of our civilisation.

At its heart lies a fundamental question: what will remain of our world?

BRASS MARKINGS AT PLACE DU CHÂTEAU

33

Strasbourg's secret meridian

Place du Château
Tram A, D – Porte-de-l'Hôpital stop – Grand'Rue stop

In the busy Place du Château, between the Musée de l'Œuvre Notre-Dame and Palais Rohan, a discreet line of brass runs diagonally across the paving. Few notice it, and fewer still know what it signifies, as there is no explanatory sign.

The broken line is made up of rectangular metal plates, each pierced with two small holes, carefully set into the grey paving stones of the square.

Leaving the cathedral forecourt and Place du Château towards the north-east, the plates are gradually replaced by small metallic squares, marking the course through narrower streets.

The line continues through Rue des Frères and Rue Fischart, eventually reaching Strasbourg's astronomical observatory on Boulevard de la Victoire, now part of the university campus.

This line represents the meridian of Strasbourg: the imaginary north-south axis that once served as the local reference for measuring longitude and time, before the Greenwich meridian was adopted as the international standard in 1884.

It was laid in 1999 as part of an artistic and heritage initiative led by the Institut de Physique du Globe de Strasbourg (IPGS) and the City of Strasbourg.

THE CHIMERA OF THE PLACE DU CHÂTEAU

34

The work of the cathedral builders, a symbol of man's work on himself

Place du Château
Trams A and D - Porte de l'Hôpital stop - Grand'Rue stop

Installed in 2013 by artisans from the Fondation de l'Œuvre Notre-Dame at the foot of the cathedral, near the Musée de l'Œuvre Notre-Dame, this monument, although highly visible, does not necessarily attract attention. Yet it houses a strange and very interesting statue discreetly nestled in a large block of sandstone. Half-animal (with its beak), half-human (the rest of the body), the creature seems to emerge from a pile of stones and leans its right hand on a cubic

stone (symbolizing the raw material shaped by the craftsman, and by extension the cathedral itself, built block by block) engraved with a symbol that is the coat of arms of the Fondation de l'Œuvre Notre-Dame (see below). In its left hand, it holds a mallet (symbolizing the tools used by craftsmen to build the cathedral). Above the cube, an open compass (symbolizing the building trades and sacred geometry) rests on the stone overlooking another mallet.

Surrounding the creature are elements of vegetation (a reminder of the importance of nature, which served as a model for medieval builders) and a lizard (a symbol of metamorphosis, resilience and rebirth), which serves as a reminder that the builder also elevated himself personally through self-improvement, while participating in the elevation of the cathedral. Stonemasons' marks are also engraved on the edges of the monument. They evoke the work of the craftsmen who contributed to the construction of the cathedral and who engraved their own symbols on the stone in order to identify their work and get paid. On the reverse side of the monument, Gothic-style bays illustrate the stages of sandstone transformation, from rough draft to finished sculpture.

In the context of cathedral construction in medieval times, this creature is actually a chimera: a hybrid creature, often monstrous, combining human and animal features.

It represents the cathedral builders: the man who shapes the rough stone to build a cathedral. But this monument has another hidden meaning: symbolically, this construction work also corresponds to the construction of a new man, to man's work on himself and his spiritual elevation through this same work. The animal part of the sculpture recalls the animal/material aspects that man must rid himself of in order to elevate himself spiritually through his work, represented by the two hammers and the compass.

The coat of arms of the Fondation de l'Œuvre Notre-Dame

A secular institution that has watched over Strasbourg Cathedral since the 13th century, the Fondation de l'Œuvre Notre-Dame is both the oldest cathedral workshop in the world and the only one still in operation in France. Its role was to finance the construction of Strasbourg Cathedral, ensure its maintenance and some of its restoration work, and collect documents relating to it. Its coat of arms consists of a cross with a triangular base that evokes stability (like the base of a building) and also symbolizes the mason's tools (such as the compass or square). It can also be interpreted as a stylized representation of the base of the cross, rooted in the earth.

STATUE OF A PROSTITUTE IN THE CATHEDRAL

35

When prostitutes visited the cathedral to sell their charms

Musée de l'Œuvre Notre-Dame
3, place du Château – 03 68 98 50 00
Tuesday to Sunday, 10am–6pm (closed 1 January, Good Friday, 1 May, 1 and 11 November, 25 December)

Among the statues in the Musée de l'Œuvre Notre-Dame is one that recalls a surprising detail of Strasbourg's history. Today, the cathedral is regarded as a solemn sanctuary where visitors are expected to dress modestly and behave respectfully. But up until the 18th century, it also served as a busy commercial space – and a place frequented by prostitutes.

Outside of mass hours, the cathedral served as a kind of covered marketplace. People came to escape the weather, often trailing in with muddy shoes and even pigs from nearby markets. Under the smoky arcades, lit by torches and candles, they sold goods in alcoves sheltered from the elements.

Prostitutes often sat on the steps leading up to the altar, facing away from the Mass, surveying the congregation for potential clients.

Although no law explicitly forbade secular activities during services, city magistrates issued numerous regulations from the second half of the 15th century (1469, 1479, 1493, 1496, 1501 and 1514) in an attempt to control prostitution.

These rules required prostitutes to wear unhemmed clothing and distinctive garments, barring them from dressing like 'respectable' women. They were also subject to fines and gradually pushed away from the cathedral.

THE WINDOW OF THE 'BESPECTACLED' EMPEROR

36

An intriguing stained-glass window

Musée de l'Œuvre Notre-Dame
3, place du Château
03 68 98 50 00
Tuesday to Sunday, 10am–6pm
Closed on 1 January, Good Friday, 1 May, 1 and 11 November and 25 December

Among the cathedral's once-numerous stained glass windows was a set portraying Holy Roman Emperors, crafted between 1176 and 1200 during the reconstruction of the Romanesque choir after the fire of 1176.

Of this series only one survives and is displayed in the museum. A stained-glass window was found in 1933 in an attic on Rue Modeste Schikelé, formerly one of the Musée de l'Œuvre Notre-Dame storerooms. The original location of this Byzantine-style majestic image is uncertain – it may have graced the north side of the cathedral or the centre of the west façade (probably the east choir). Other windows depicting the emperors and kings who ruled Alsace before 1250 are on the north aisle of the Romanesque cathedral.

The identity of the so-called 'bespectacled' emperor has never been established. He has been variously considered as Charlemagne, as the Germanic emperor Henry II (both canonised in the 12th century), as King Solomon, or simply as a symbol of power. Given that the halo (nimbus) is usually reserved for saints, the Charlemagne or Henry II hypotheses are the most plausible. But since Charlemagne was canonised in 1165 by the antipope Pascal III, a measure that the Roman Curia never formally recognised (nor invalidated), many scholars favour Henry II. Renowned for his piety and his role in Church reform, Henry II was the only Germanic emperor to be officially canonised (1146). Finally, the red halo (see below) seems to be more Henry II than Charlemagne.

Why does this emperor appear to be wearing glasses?

The appearance of spectacles is a by-product of stained-glass technique. The craftsmen used grey tones and black lead lines around the eyes to add depth and realism, unintentionally creating the impression of eyewear.

Why is the emperor's nimbus red?

While halos are traditionally gold or yellow to evoke divine light, medieval artisans sometimes used liturgical colours: white for purity, blue for the heavens, red for martyrdom and charity, green for hope, and purple for humility and penance.

PAINTING OF 'THE DEAD LOVERS'

37

A spectacular message on the vanity of earthly things, sin and sexuality

Musée de l'Œuvre Notre-Dame
3, place du Château
Tuesday to Friday 10am–1pm and 2pm–6pm, Saturday and Sunday 10am–6pm

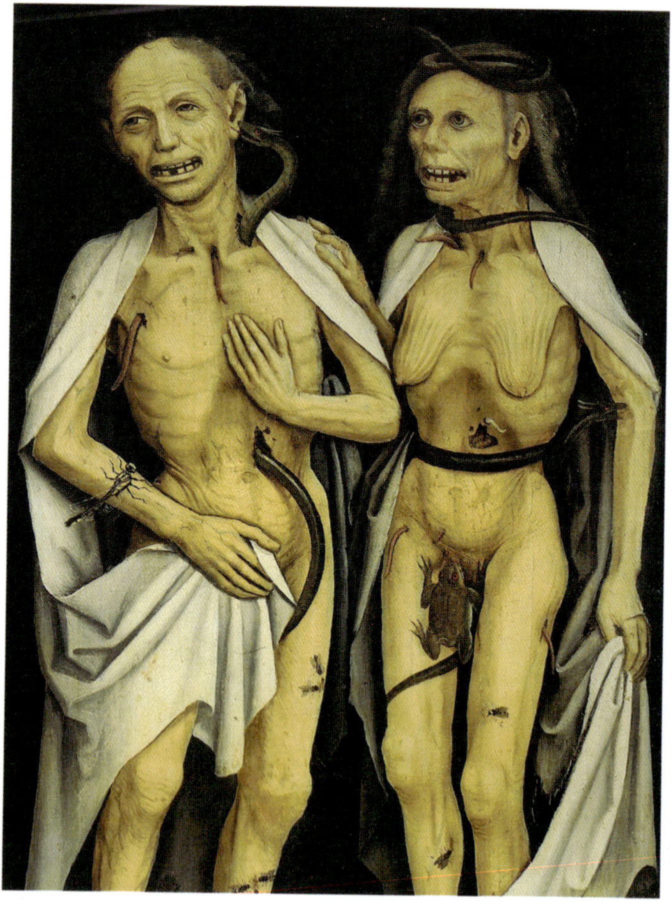

At the Musée de l'Œuvre Notre-Dame hangs the striking 'The Dead Lovers' ('Les amants trépassés'), painted around 1470 by an anonymous artist known as the Master of Ulm.

The work offers a chilling vision of two decomposing elderly bodies – a man and a woman, fully naked, standing side by side in near-total darkness, framed only by pale drapes.

Their wax-like skin is streaked with wounds and nests of vermin. Snakes coil around their necks, piercing their entrails.

A toad squats on the woman's genitals, while swarms of insects feed on their flesh.

Each creature carries symbolic weight: the snake, long linked with sin and lust, here embodies corruption and decay; the fly, medieval emblem of defilement and mortality; the dragonfly, a reminder of life's brevity and the illusion of earthly pleasures. The toad, imagined in the Middle Ages as the epitome of lust, directly indicts female sexuality – considered the ultimate source of sin.

Yet, amid this anatomical horror, the spouses remain alive: the woman's hand rests tenderly on her companion's shoulder, a lingering gesture of intimacy.

The painting belongs to the German late Gothic tradition, its morbid naturalism recalling the engravings of the 'Master of the Book of Reason' in the 15th century.

Originally, it formed one half of a diptych: the other panel, now housed at the Cleveland Museum of Art (Ohio), depicts the same couple alive – youthful, elegant, richly dressed, surrounded by plants symbolising love, fertility, innocence and modesty.

The juxtaposition of the two panels confronts viewers with a stark meditation on the vanity of earthly pleasures, the inevitability of death, and the urgency of living well while preparing for the hereafter.

The Strasbourg panel may even suggest, much like the corrupted portrait in 'The Picture of Dorian Gray', that the couple's flesh betrays the spiritual failings of their earthly life.

'LES CIMETIÈRES DES NAUFRAGÉS' (38)

A discreet artwork for those who don't usually have a grave

Place du Château – Garden of Musée de l'Œuvre-Notre-Dame
Visible from outside
Tram A, D – Porte de l'Hôpital stop – Grand'Rue stop

Through a gate on the narrow Hans Haug passage, between Place du Château and Rue du Maroquin, you can glimpse the charming little garden of the Musée de l'Œuvre-Notre-Dame. The only way to

enter, however, is through the museum itself.

Here, tucked among the leaves, medicinal plants, and numerous steles and tombstones, lies a little-known artwork. Gradually falling into oblivion, like the very sailors it commemorates, the piece often escapes the attention of visitors.

Created by Ian Hamilton Finlay in 1988 and entitled 'Les Cimetières des Naufragés / Symbolisme' ('Graveyards of the Shipwrecked / Symbolism'), the artwork evokes the idea of maritime burials – symbolic resting places for sailors lost at sea.

Unlike a traditional cemetery, the shipwrecked often have no physical grave; their remains are entrusted to the sea.

Finlay's work is a simple slab of pink sandstone, engraved with its name, recalling the medieval tombstones surrounding it. The choice of typically Alsatian material creates a link between this modern creation and local history.

The idea of the sea as a natural tomb recurs throughout history and literature, evoking both its protective immensity and its destructive power. Finlay's piece pays tribute to the countless anonymous sailors who perished at sea, never receiving a traditional burial.

By including the word 'Symbolisme' in the title, Finlay references the artistic movement of the late 19th century, whose key principles included the suggestion of absent realities and the symbolic use of natural elements – such as the sea, death, and memory – to evoke emotional and mystical resonance. The artist doesn't depict the shipwrecked, but rather their absence. He doesn't erect a traditional stele, but offers a simple inscription – a symbolic trace, the only tangible form of remembrance.

This approach is reminiscent of Symbolist poetry, which relied on implicit meaning to evoke sensations and emotions. The artwork, accompanied by creeping ivy (a classic symbol of memory and eternity), echoes ancient cemeteries where nature eventually reclaims its space among tombs and monuments.

Integrated into a museum steeped in history, the work forms a bridge between past and present, reinforcing the notion of a natural cycle in which memories of the lost gradually fade. The simplicity of the installation enhances the evocative power of its artistic language.

SAINT JAMES' SCALLOP SHELL NEAR THE CATHEDRAL (39)

A stage on the Way of Saint James

At the corner of Place de la Cathédrale and the Rue du Maroquin

Hidden in plain sight, a discreet, scallop-shaped stone lies embedded among the cobblestones at the corner of Place de la Cathédrale and Rue du Maroquin. Installed in July 2013, this small detail commemorates Strasbourg's role as one of the historic starting points for pilgrims setting out on the Way of Saint James – a journey symbolised by the scallop shell.

Pilgrims traditionally followed major trade routes frequented by merchants and travellers from the Holy Roman Empire, France, the Netherlands, Switzerland and Savoy. The Strasbourg 'tribe' of boatmen (see p. 87) provided crossings of the Rhine, while the city offered easy access to the mountain passes of the Vosges, leading west.

This pilgrimage route also became a symbol of reconciliation in Franco-German relations. In 1987, the Council of Europe recognised the Camino de Santiago as its very first European Cultural Route (see below). Then in 1993, UNESCO inscribed these ancient paths on the World Heritage List 'to promote intellectual, educational, artistic and cultural exchanges between regions and nations.'

The pilgrimage still inspires modern travellers: every year, nearly 200,000 people embark on this journey in one form or another.

Traditionally, pilgrims collect the scallop shell at the end of the route, fastening it to their clothing or backpack as a sign of completion.

The phrase 'Way of the Stars' refers to a popular medieval legend about a 'shower of stars in the sky,' which supposedly guided a hermit to discover the tomb of Saint James in Santiago around 813. Although no historical evidence supports the story, what was discovered in the 9th century was more likely a simple burial mound from a Roman cemetery.

Strasbourg: the 'City of Roads'

Strasbourg's very name means 'the city of roads.' The German *Straßburg* combines *Straße* (road) and *Burg* (fortified settlement), reflecting the city's origins. From this, locals have affectionately coined the Alsatian nicknames *Strossburi* or *Stroßbùrri.*

WEATHERVANE AT PLACE DU MARCHÉ-AUX-COCHONS-DE-LAIT

40

Legend of Hungarian Emperor Sigismund's shoe

1, place du Marché-aux-Cochons-de-Lait
Tram A, D – Porte-de-l'Hôpital stop

In the heart of Strasbourg, a discreet but fascinating architectural detail has stood watch for centuries on Place du Marché-aux-Cochons-de-Lait. At the top of the roof of No. 1, an intriguing shoe-shaped weathervane attracts curious looks. As a silent witness to the past, it tells local history through legend and craftsmanship.

The house that carries this weathervane is itself a local heritage gem. The ground floor dates from 1477, as attested by an inscription on the corner.

Converted in 1606 and raised higher in 1612, the building still retains its original wooden panels. It once belonged to a shoemaker whose initials, 'HWE', are engraved on the façade and on the weathervane itself.

The vane represents a poulaine shoe (see opposite) in metal, its long-curved toe characteristic of the Middle Ages – a piece of both art and tradition. A decorative scroll at the back adds elegance, while its vertical axis is topped with a wrought-iron ornament, typical of historic weathervanes.

According to legend, the shoe recalls an episode from 1414. During a stay in Strasbourg, Emperor Sigismund of Hungary, carried away by dancing at a reception, is said to have forgotten his shoes.

Aware of his discomfort, several noble ladies led him to a local shoemaker – at this very address – to buy a new pair. In gratitude, Sigismund granted the artisan the privilege of marking his shop with a sign in the shape of a shoe, commemorating the unusual event.

What is a poulaine?

Recognisable by its elongated, tapered toe, the poulaine shoe is one of the most emblematic medieval fashion accessories. Originating in the 14th century, it reached its peak in the 15th century at European courts.

The origins of the shoe remain a matter of debate. Some historians trace it to Poland – hence its name – before it gained popularity in France and England through trade and royal alliances. Others suggest it was inspired by footwear worn by Mongolian or Persian riders in the Near East.

Originally favoured by urban elites, the length of the toe reflected the wearer's status: the longer the toe, the more powerful the owner appeared. Oversized poulaines suggested that their wearer didn't need to walk far – a symbol of wealth and privilege.

Yet faced with increasingly extravagant lengths, the Church condemned the fashion as a mark of pride and frivolity. Royal edicts attempted to regulate the excesses: under Charles V of France, for example, the bourgeoisie were forbidden from wearing the longest versions, which were reserved for aristocrats.

On the battlefield, the impracticality of these shoes became apparent: soldiers were sometimes forced to cut off the tips before going to war.

By the late 15th century, poulaines had fallen out of fashion in favour of more functional footwear with wide, square tips. Their disappearance reflected not only changes in fashion but also a shift in social attitudes and a move towards simpler male attire.

SYMBOLS OF POST CORNER OF 1, RUE DES CORDIERS

(41)

Superstition engraved on wood

1, rue des Cordiers

At No. 1, rue des Cordiers, on the corner of the half-timbered house that is now part of the Musée de l'OEuvre-Notre-Dame, on the first floor, there is a curious symbol engraved in a wooden cartouche. It features (from top to bottom) a five-pointed star (a pentagram, see double page opposite), the monogram HIF (the initials of the owner, now unknown) and a hatchet.

This cartouche is surmounted by a second cartouche bearing the date 1672.

Located in plain view from the street, this corner post (known as a 'cornier' post in Alsatian tradition, see below) traditionally displays the status of its owner for all to see.

The pentagram also has an apotropaic function here: it protects against the evil eye and all kinds of harmful and evil influences (see next double page). In particular, it was supposed to defend the house against lightning, fire, and witches.

The hatchet indicates the owner's profession: a butcher who certainly belonged to the Poële de la Fleur, the city's butchers' guild.

Corner posts

One of the characteristic features of Alsatian houses is the corner post, located at the corners of the buildings.
The roof structure and the vertical posts on the four walls rest on these posts. In Alsace, unlike other regions where half-timbered houses are found, there is a balance between vertical, horizontal, and diagonal beams.

Earlobe-shaped motifs

On either side of the engraved symbol are cartilage-style motifs, which were very popular in the Rhineland in the 17th century. They are also called auricular motifs because they resemble the shape of a human earlobe.

For more information on the five-pointed star (pentagram), see the following double page.

Rue des Cordiers (street of rope makers) has been known by this name since the first half of the 14th century. In previous centuries, it was called Rue du Lin (Flax Street): ropes were very often made from flax or hemp. The region also produced large quantities of these materials and traded them extensively through the old port of Strasbourg, which was also a major consumer of rope.

The symbolism of the pentragram, the five-pointed star

The pentagram is a five-pointed star composed of five straight lines. In Portuguese, *pentagrama* means a word with five letters.

In music, it is also the five parallel lines that compose sheet music. Originally, it was the symbol of the Roman goddess Venus and, consequently, was associated with this planet as its orbit, as seen from Earth, apparently draws a five-pointed star every eight years, as illustrated by the astronomer Ptolemy.

In nature, the pentagram is the sign of the fifth element, Ether, which occupies the superior branch, while the other four elements (Air, Fire, Water, Earth) occupy the inferior branches.

The pentagram (or pentalpha) is also the symbol for Infinity. In the pentagon at the centre of the pentagram, another smaller pentagram can be drawn, and so on. It also possesses a numerical symbolism, always based on the number 5, which represents the marriage between the masculine (3) and the feminine (2), and thus symbolises the union of opposites that is necessary for spiritual realisation. That is why, in the mathematics of the Pythagorean school of thought, the pentagram (the emblem of this Greek institution) is linked to the golden ratio (1.618). Composed of a regular pentagon and five isosceles triangles, the ratio between the side of the triangle and its base (the side of the pentagon) is equal to the golden number.

The Jewish Kabbalah, through its most learned rabbis, considers the pentagram to be the symbol of the will of God and of divine protection.

In Christianity, it is the star of Christmas and of Christ's birth, which predicts the Resurrection of both the spirit in the body (birth) and the body in the spirit (resurrection).

In Freemasonry, it is the Blazing Star of initiation. Placed in the eastern part of the Lodge, it also symbolises the resurrection, when the follower leaves the profane world to become a new initiate.

When the pentagram is shown upside down, it generally becomes a symbol of Evil, the opposite of what it symbolises when upright (Good). It means that the Spirit has been plunged into the blindness of Matter and the physical suffering of the human soul.

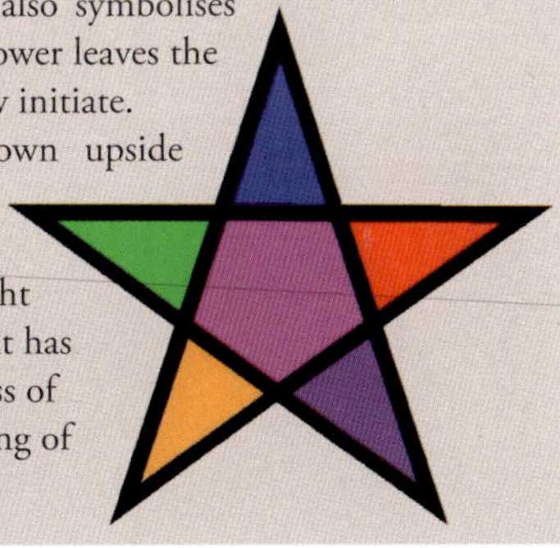

RELIEF OF THE GOD MITHRAS

42

An extraordinary reconstitution of a Roman relief

Archaeological Museum
Palais des Rohan
2, place du Château
03 68 98 50 00
Wednesday to Monday, 10am–6pm

In the section of the Archaeological Museum entitled Five Centuries of Gallo-Roman Civilisation in Alsace, a surprising-coloured relief depicts a man wearing a toga and a red Phrygian cap struggling with a bull. Numerous figures and details surround the scene.

Dated to the 2nd century CE, this depiction of the god Mithras is a spectacular reconstruction of a four-metre-high relief originally discovered in 1911 on Rue du Schockeloch in the Koenigshoffen district during the construction of St Paul's Church. Excavations carried out on the site by archaeologist Robert Forrer (1866–1947) confirmed the presence of a mithraeum here. The present-day Koenigshoffen, once a Gallo-Roman vicus adjoining the legionary camp of Strasbourg-Argentorate, included a shrine dedicated to Mithras, with a carved altarpiece, votive reliefs, an altar flanked by lions and benches for the faithful.

The Koenigshoffen relief was one of the largest known in the Roman world. It was polychrome, as confirmed by a dedication made by a soldier named C. Celsinius Matutinus, who paid to have it repainted during the reign of Emperor Severus Alexander (222–235). The sanctuary appears to have been abandoned after its destruction in the mid-3rd century CE, possibly by the first Christian communities of Strasbourg.

Mithraism, or the cult of Mithras – an Indo-Iranian deity attested as early as the 2nd millennium BCE (see following double-page spread) – was particularly widespread among Roman soldiers and merchants. This explains the presence of a mithraeum close to the legionary camp of Strasbourg-Argentorate.

On the relief in the Archaeological Museum, Mithras is shown slaughtering a bull, surrounded by a scorpion, a snake and a dog – symbols integral to the mythology of this ancient cult.

For more on Mithraism, see following double-page spread.

Mithraism – a fascinating ancient cult for initiates

Mithraism was a religious cult centred around Mithras, a god of Iranian origin.
Born from a rock, Mithras emerged naked, armed with a knife, holding a torch in one hand and wearing a Phrygian cap.
After vanquishing the sun, he signed a pact with his former adversary and received a radiant crown – his new emblem.
Pursuing evil, Mithras, aided by his faithful dog, captured a bull – symbolising wild, untamed forces – and killed it. From the bull's marrow, wheat miraculously sprang forth, while its blood gave rise to a vine, as if death were a prerequisite for rebirth.
But Ahriman, the god of evil, sought revenge: he sent a scorpion and a snake to foil Mithras' triumph, but they failed. Mithras and the sun celebrated their victory with an agape – a sacred feast, a word that has remained in modern vocabulary.
Mithraic ceremonies typically took place in caves or underground temples, not out of an attachment to darkness, as some critics later claimed, but because the cave symbolised the cosmos, the ultimate destination of this spiritual path.
Mithras was accompanied by two torchbearers: Cautes and Cautopates, forming a triad (or trinity). One bore a raised, lit torch symbolising day, the other a lowered, extinguished one symbolising night. These two figures were simply representations of Mithras himself.
The journey of the soul through the cosmos was at the heart of the Mithraic faith. Devotees progressed along this path through seven stages, corresponding to the seven planets, the seven days of the week, seven metals and seven states of the soul, which had to be gradually transcended.
The cult offered a way to progress on this journey, to free oneself from worldly passions.

The feast – or *agape* – based on bread and wine, recalled the Eucharist; while the slaying of the bull, from which new life emerged, evoked the ideas of sacrifice and resurrection.
Spreading across the Roman world from the 1st century BCE, Mithraism reached its peak in the 3rd century CE, before gradually giving way to Christianity.

Christmas owes its date of 25 December to Mithraism

Contrary to popular belief, no Christian text confirms that Jesus was born on the night of 24–25 December.

In 354, Pope Liberius fixed this date for celebrating Christmas to combat pagan Roman cults – especially Mithraism, which celebrated Mithras' birth on the winter solstice, traditionally 25 December (before the Gregorian calendar reform, the solstice was not fixed to 21 December – one of the reasons for the Gregorian calendar's introduction).

By reclaiming this date, the Church created a profound symbol: at the time of year when nights were longest, the birth of Christ signified the rising of a new day, light dispelling darkness, and the promise of resurrection.

Before this change, Christians had celebrated Christ's birth on 6 January, the same day as the Adoration of the Magi.

Only the Armenian Apostolic Church still celebrates Christmas on this date, while some Orthodox churches observe it on what corresponds to 25 December in the Julian calendar. Incidentally, tradition suggests that Jesus was not born in year 0 but rather in 5 or 7 BCE.

HOUSES AT Nos. 2 AND 4, IMPASSE DE LA BIÈRE

43

The oldest houses in Strasbourg

2 and 4, impasse de la Bière

The oldest houses in Strasbourg are hidden away in a little-known alleyway, the Impasse de la Bière. These two adjoining buildings, numbers 2 and 4, were listed as Historic Monuments in 1971. Although they are still inhabited, and therefore private, they can be admired from the outside.

Built in the late Gothic style, these houses date from the 15th and 16th centuries. The ground floors of the twin houses are accessed through a door set within a Gothic sandstone arch. The door and window frames on this level are all made of Vosges stone. The three upper levels, with their corbelled construction, are timber framed, partially concealed by an exterior render (see below).

Beer for the Cathedral workers

The name of the alleyway dates back to at least 1302. It was named Impasse de la Bière because a brewer set up there in 1259, in a building that has since been destroyed. His name was Master Arnold, and he was the first professional brewer in the city to hold the title of Master. Situated close to the cathedral building site, his brewery delighted the workers with this nourishing drink.

Timber-framed houses

Old Alsatian houses – and those of Strasbourg in particular – are often mistakenly called 'half-timbered houses.' Half-timbering refers to the vertical beams or joists in a structure.

In Alsace, however, the beams are usually positioned at an angle to provide greater stability in the event of seismic tremors, as the region is located on a well-known fault line.

Unlike half-timbering, timber framing creates a structure in which all the elements are interconnected. Its fundamental principle is that of balance and stability, using triangular forms deemed incapable of being deformed.

When the nearby town of Basel was destroyed by an earthquake in 1356, the few houses that survived were those built using timber frame construction.

The spaces between the beams were filled with cob, sometimes covered with render. Timber-framed houses could also be disassembled and moved elsewhere.

THE MIKVEH IN THE OLD JEWISH QUARTER

44

A 14th-century ritual bath discovered by chance

20, rue des Charpentiers
Accessible on a few selected days each year ; guided tours possible
Contact the City of Strasbourg's Department of Culture for more information: strasbourg.eu/contact-direction-culture
03 68 98 72 77

Despite the massacre of Strasbourg's Jewish community in 1349 (see the following double-page spread), the city has preserved several Jewish heritage sites. Since at least 1587, the Rue des Juifs (see p. 193) and its surrounding alleys were known orally as *Zum Judenbad* ('At the Jewish bath').

However, the mikveh itself remained hidden until 1985, when renovation work at the corner of Rue des Juifs (no. 15) and Rue des Charpentiers (nos. 20 and 22) led to an archaeological discovery: a 14th-century ritual bath, once part of a synagogue.

The structure is a square sandstone room, about 3 metres wide, topped with a barrel-vaulted ceiling in red brick. Four Romanesque stone brackets mark the corners beneath the vault.

The central basin, supplied by the water table, may also have received rainwater through a circular zenithal opening in the ceiling, 0.90 metres in diameter.

The remains can be seen of a sandstone staircase that led from the basin entrance, at ground level, to the water table.

Part of these steps were probably reused to build a well, which replaced the ritual bath after the expulsion of the Jews from Strasbourg. This well was also unearthed during the excavations.

Intriguingly, the opening discovered on this occasion did not align with the vault's zenithal opening.

The work of clearing thc site of the ritual bath exposed the base of the well, made up of four large slabs about 1 metre wide, 1.3 metres high and 12 cm thick.

What is a mikveh ?

In Judaism, a *mikveh* is a ritual bath used for purification, particularly in the context of family purity. It holds the same communal importance as the synagogue and yeshiva (Jewish school).

The massacre of the Jews of Strasbourg, accused of having caused the Black Death of 1347

The Black Death appeared in 1347 and over five years killed 30–50% of the European population – about 25 million people. Rumours spread around the continent that the Jews had triggered the epidemic by poisoning wells ...

Accused of having caused this catastrophe, Strasbourg's Jewish community was completely wiped out.

On 14 February 1349 all Jews in the city were transported to their own cemetery (in what is now Place de la République) to be burned alive at the scaffold.

The Black Death, so-called because of dark spots on the skin caused by internal bleeding (septicemia), swiftly spread along the inland waterways from Genoa, ravaging trading cities such as Strasbourg. Doctors were unable to control the outbreak and a grim pessimism took over, leading to the idea of purification by looking for scapegoats. Jews, who seemed to be less affected by the plague than others, largely because their strict hygiene rituals protected them, were the ideal target. They were thought to be dumping poison and venom into wells and rivers to eliminate Christians.

Everywhere in Europe Jews were accused, and under torture some confessed to crimes they hadn't committed. In Strasbourg the wells were sealed and the Jewish quarter (around Rue des Juifs) condemned.

The mayor, Ammeister Peter Schwarber, denounced these claims as false, but his opponents saw a chance to unseat him and take office. Until then the city's Jews had been money-lenders, one of the few roles available to them but not to Christians.

Over time the clergy and nobility contracted heavy debts towards the Jewish community, and an assembly of nobles planned to exterminate the Jews or convert them under the pretext of fighting the plague.

Schwarber tried to save them, but he was accused of corruption, exiled from the city and his wealth confiscated. It was reported at the time that 2,000 Jews were executed, although historians believe the community numbered closer to 1,000.

From 1388 until the French Revolution, Jews were banned from living in Strasbourg and had to leave the city by 7pm each day. A horn blown from the cathedral platform signalled their curfew.

The Rue des Juifs

Originally built along the Roman cardo (east-west axis), the Rue des Juifs is among Strasbourg's oldest streets, and by the 12th century had a thriving Jewish community.

The street included a synagogue (no. 30), a bakery (no. 17), a prison (no. 9), a mikveh (no. 20, rue des Charpentiers), and a cemetery (now Place de la République).

The Gothic house at no. 15, built in 1290, is the last surviving building from the medieval Jewish quarter.

In the 16th century, it became the Hôtel des Joham de Mundolsheim, home to a wealthy family of merchants and bankers.

PLAQUE COMMEMORATING THE BLACK HAND

Teenagers who defied the Third Reich

Façade of Saint Stephen's Episcopal College
2, rue de la Pierre Large

In 2008, a moving commemorative plaque was affixed to the façade of Saint Stephen's Episcopal College, honouring around 20 young heroes. It was here, in September 1940, that 16-year-old apprentice draftsman Marcel Weinum founded a resistance movement with his schoolmates. Known as the 'Black Hand', the group comprised teenagers aged 14 to 16.

Despite their youth – and the fact that most acted without their parents' knowledge – the Black Hand quickly attracted the attention of the German authorities.

From October 1940, subversive slogans and crosses of Lorraine began to appear across Strasbourg. Nazi flags were torn down during the night. In November, the group sabotaged Wehrmacht telephone wires and railway transmission cables.

By December, they were smashing windows that displayed portraits of Hitler. Within weeks, the Führer's image had vanished from shopfronts – despite shopkeepers being fined.

The group began building an arsenal, looting weapons from abandoned Maginot Line forts, official vehicles, and even Nazi offices. By May 1941, they were capable of launching attacks. On the evening of 8 May, Weinum and comrade Uhlrich destroyed the car of Gauleiter Robert Wagner near Place Karl-Roos (now Place Kléber, see p. 25).

The Black Hand also established contact with the British consulate in Basel. But on the evening of 20 May 1941, Weinum and fellow member Ceslav Sieradzki were arrested by customs officers en route to Basel by bike – caught with airfield plans for Entzheim and Haguenau. By July, the Black Hand had ceased to exist.

After brutal torture, Sieradzki was executed by gunshot to the neck on 12 December 1941. Other members were imprisoned at Schirmeck before being forcibly conscripted into the German army. Marcel Weinum, then only 18, was beheaded in Stuttgart on 14 April 1942, having refused to cooperate. The words inscribed on the plaque come from his final letter to his parents: 'If I must die, I die with a pure heart.'

ST ATTALA'S HAND

46

The extraordinary epic of the one-handed relic

Collège épiscopal Saint-Étienne
2, rue de la Pierre Large
Open only during Heritage Days

The renowned Saint-Étienne episcopal college, accessible only during Heritage Days, conceals one of Strasbourg's greatest treasures, still unknown to most residents.

On the right-hand side of the college church choir, the mummified hand of St Attala, first Abbess of Strasbourg (c. 690–741) and niece of St Odilia of Alsace, is preserved in a rock-crystal reliquary.

When Attala died in 741, her body was displayed, as was customary, in the abbey church of Saint-Étienne, built in the 8th century on the site of today's college. Pilgrims flocked to pay their final tribute, and rumours of miraculous cures quickly spread, drawing crowds to the abbey.

According to tradition, Werentrude, Abbess of Hohenbourg and successor to St Odilia, was consumed by jealousy. She ordered her emissary Werner to steal a keepsake from the deceased during the night. He could have chosen garments or objects, but instead took the saint's hand.

Armed with the relic, Werner fled through Strasbourg's streets but became lost. By dawn he found himself once again in front of the abbey church of Saint-Étienne, where his theft was discovered and the hand retrieved – except for the thumb, which he was allowed to deliver to his patron.

The story of the relic did not end there. Two centuries later, the Bishop of Strasbourg Widerolfus sought to seize it, resenting the pilgrimage that diverted the faithful to Saint-Étienne abbey at the expense of his own church.

A deacon, warned by divine revelation, learned of the bishop's plan and, in desperation, hid both the body and relic.

Another 250 years passed before they were rediscovered. In 1172, when construction began on the new Saint-Étienne church (completed in 1175), an old man claiming to be a seer revealed that they lay hidden in a well beneath the church (still visible today).

To ensure its safety, the hand was placed in a magnificent rock-crystal reliquary, a masterpiece of medieval lapidary, where it remains on display.

Tapestry showing St Attala's hand

A large wool and linen tapestry, over four metres long, was created in 1440 to commemorate the tumultuous journey of St Attala's hand. The hanging illustrates her life, the nocturnal theft of her relic, its concealment, and its liturgical triumph. The work survives in two fragments, now preserved at the Musée de l'Œuvre Notre-Dame.

EFFIGY OF A DOG

47

Dog grooming, turn-of-the-century style

11, rue des Bains
Municipal Baths of Strasbourg
bainsmunicipauxdestrasbourg.fr
Timetables on the website

Few passers-by notice the charming effigy of a dog sitting up and begging on the metal railings outside no. 11, rue des Bains. Yet this little sculpture marks the original entrance to the old dog baths, once attached to the Municipal Baths of Strasbourg.

Built between 1904 and 1911 by Fritz Beblo, Strasbourg's municipal architect – and also a Prussian artist – the Municipal Baths were designed to meet the urgent hygiene needs of a rapidly growing city. Strasbourg's population doubled between 1871 and 1905, and with most homes lacking private bathrooms, the need for public bathing facilities had become pressing.

The impressive complex offered a variety of facilities, divided by purpose and clientele: large swimming pools for men, separate pools for women, Roman baths with steam rooms, medical and hydrotherapy rooms, showers, a solarium, a boiler room – and, less well known, baths for dogs.

These dog baths are the most forgotten feature of an establishment still popular today. The effigy on the railings – a long-haired poodle with a small goatee and drooping ears – was designed by Beblo himself.

Dogs of all shapes and sizes were brought by their owners to scheduled appointments, where they were washed and groomed by trained staff. Each dog was placed in an earthenware basin and scrubbed with soap and clean water before being rinsed and passed through a revolutionary steam room that left them clean and dry. While waiting for their owners to collect them, the dogs were tethered to the wall with small chains and provided with bowls of fresh water. Prices varied depending on the dog's size and the length of its hair. This unusual service finally disappeared in 1969.

INSCRIPTION AT THEATRUM ANATOMICUM

Reminder of Strasbourg's medical history

1, place de l'Hôpital
Tram A, D – Porte de l'Hôpital stop

A marble inscription, discreetly fixed above a walled-up doorway at 1 Place de l'Hôpital, sometimes catches the eye of attentive passers-by.

The partially erased text, framed with rocaille volutes and topped by a carved shell, reads: *Theatrum Anatomicum … Et Procerum Munificentia Ornatum Instructum Marmore Hoc Ornat Grata Hygea Anno MDCCXL.* It translates as: 'The anatomical theatre … decorated and equipped thanks to the munificence of notables, is adorned with this marble by grateful Hygea, in the year 1740.'

Here, Hygea refers to the goddess of health. The inscription is a rare testimony to a place long hidden from the public: Strasbourg's anatomical theatre.

This section of the old Gothic chapel of Saint-Erhard, attached to the hospital, was used between 1670 and 1878 for the teaching of anatomy.

The chapel, converted into a lecture room, was fitted with tiered seating so students could observe dissections in a setting that was solemn and deliberately private, reflecting the secrecy that surrounded such practices at the time, reserved for a restricted circle of doctors and scholars.

Built between 1396 and 1428, the Saint-Erhard chapel, supported by powerful buttresses and pierced with Gothic ogival windows, has survived the centuries. Partially destroyed by the fire of 1716, it still preserves much of its original architecture.

It was in this medieval setting that modern anatomy took shape in Strasbourg, paving the way for the major medical advances of the 19th century.

'GOETHE 1770' inscription

Beneath the evocation of the anatomical theatre, another modern inscription – 'GOETHE 1770' – recalls the presence of the writer Johann Wolfgang von Goethe in Strasbourg (see p. 141 to 143). Arriving in 1770 to study law, the young Goethe also attended the university and took anatomy lessons in this building.

The same inscription can be found several times on the chapel's outer walls.

ANIMAL PAVILION FRIEZE

49

Dog and rabbits: reminder of the pavilion's former function

Hôpital Civil
6am–10pm
Tram A, D – Étoile Bourse stop – Porte de l'Hôpital stop

The animal pavilion holds a special place within the Hôpital Civil. Built in 1921 in the gardens of the Faculty of Medicine's Institute of Haematology, it was once used to breed animals for medical experiments.

The reinforced concrete building, designed by the University of Strasbourg's chief architect Patrice Bonnet, adopts a style known as 'picturesque romanticism', reminiscent of the Arts and Crafts movement.

One of its most striking features is the carved frieze on the south façade, showing rabbits among swirling foliage – a discreet reminder of the building's former purpose in biomedical research.

Beneath this frieze, a sculpted dog's head can be interpreted either as an allegory of vigilance and loyalty or as a reference to the role of dogs in medical research at the time.

Over the years, medical practices evolved. Animal testing was gradually moved to modern facilities meeting stricter health standards, and animals (especially mice) were transferred to dedicated spaces in the Haematology building.

The animal pavilion itself was later restored and converted into offices, but the original sculptures and architectural style have been preserved.

© Roland Burckel

The Hôpital Civil, one of Strasbourg's most symbolic institutions, has a history dating back to 1398. Today, it comprises 45 buildings spread across some 23 hectares. Although much of the site was destroyed by fire in 1716, several old structures survived.
Architectural changes continued over the centuries. Between 1717 and 1725, a new hospital was constructed, blending elements of the Rhenish Renaissance with French influences. The 19th century saw further extensions, followed by the construction of several medical institutes while the city was under German rule.

Scandal of the remains of a dead elephant in coffins

The most disturbing episode in the hospital's history is the story of the circus elephant that died in the summer of 1897. The remains were coveted by Professor G. Schwalbe, who bought the carcass for anatomical study. However, in the intense summer heat, decomposition set in quickly, making dissection impossible. Faced with this grim situation, professors and students took a decision as pragmatic as it was unspeakable: they disposed of the remains by placing them in coffins meant for people awaiting burial.
The scheme was exposed when rumours spread among the gravediggers, puzzled by the unusual weight of certain coffin. The scandal forced the university to issue an official apology.

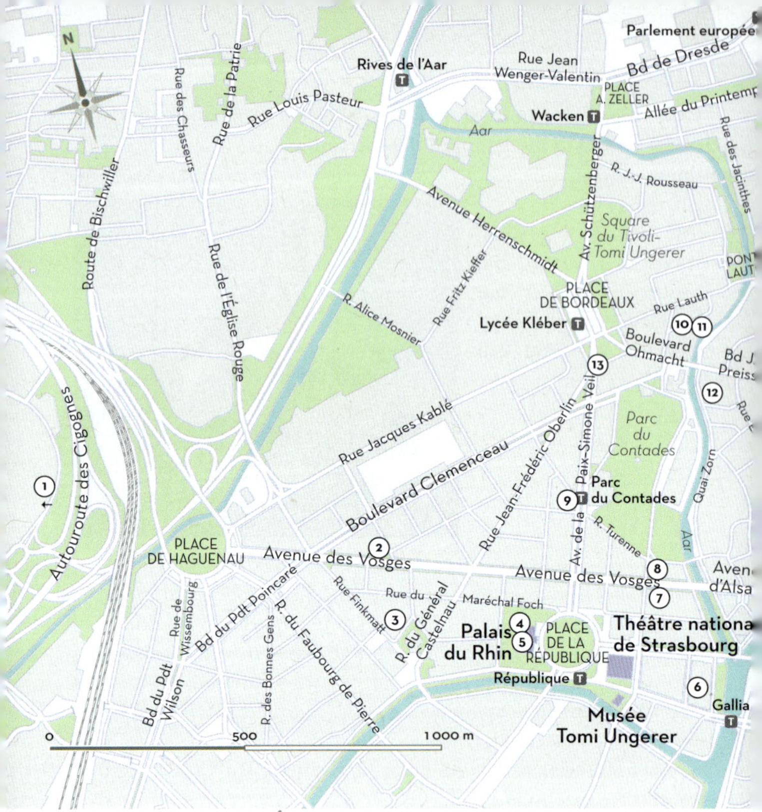
N
Parlement europée
Rives de l'Aar
Rue Jean Wenger-Valentin
Bd de Dresde
PLACE A. ZELLER
Allée du Printemp
Wacken
Rue Louis Pasteur
Rue des Chasseurs
Rue de la Patrie
Aar
R. J.-J. Rousseau
Rue des Jacinthes
Avenue Herrenschmidt
Av. Schützenberger
Square du Tivoli-Tomi Ungerer
Route de Bischwiller
Rue de l'Église Rouge
Rue Fritz Kieffer
R. Alice Mosnier
PLACE DE BORDEAUX
Lycée Kléber
Rue Lauth
Boulevard Ohmacht
Bd J. Preiss
Autouroute des Cigognes
Rue Jacques Kablé
Rue Jean-Frédéric Oberlin
Av. de la Paix-Simone Veil
Parc du Contades
Parc du Contades
Quai Zorn
Boulevard Clemenceau
R. Turenne
Aar
PLACE DE HAGUENAU
Avenue des Vosges
Avenue des Vosges
Aven d'Alsa
Rue de Wissembourg
Bd du Pdt Poincaré
Rue Finkmatt
Rue du Maréchal Foch
R. du Général Castelnau
Palais du Rhin
PLACE DE LA RÉPUBLIQUE
Théâtre nationa de Strasbourg
République
R. des Bonnes Gens
R. du Faubourg de Pierre
Bd du Pdt Wilson
Gallia
Musée Tomi Ungerer
0
500
1 000 m

Neustadt

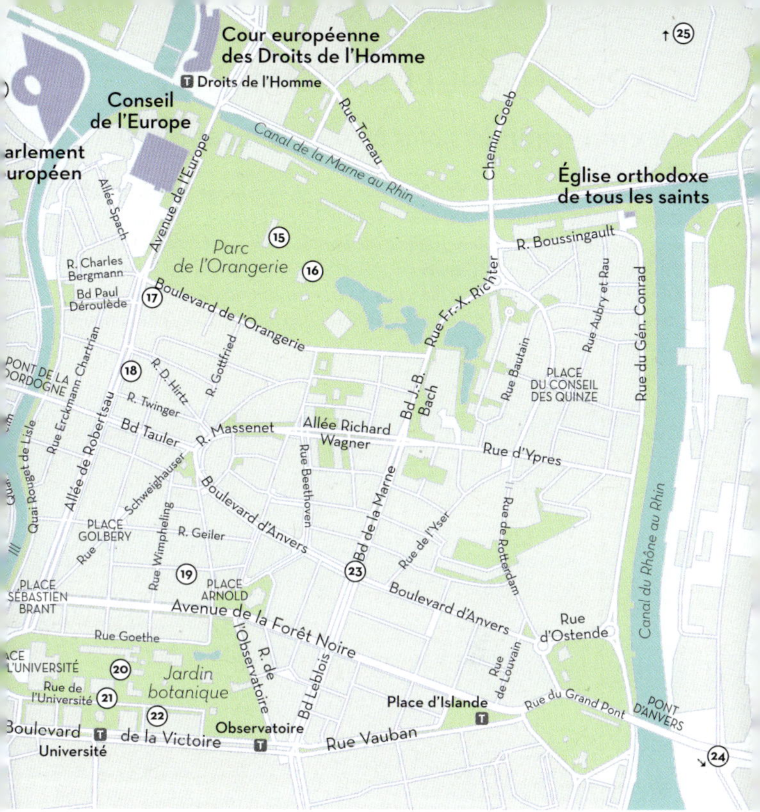
Cour européenne des Droits de l'Homme
Droits de l'Homme
Conseil de l'Europe
arlement uropéen
Église orthodoxe de tous les saints
Canal de la Marne au Rhin
Rue Toreau
Chemin Goeb
Avenue de l'Europe
Allée Spach
Parc de l'Orangerie
R. Boussingault
R. Charles Bergmann
Bd Paul Déroulède
Boulevard de l'Orangerie
Rue Fr.-X. Richter
Rue Aubry et Rau
Rue du Gén. Conrad
PONT DE LA DORDOGNE
Rue Erckmann Chartrian
R. D. Hirtz
R. Gottfried
Rue Bautain
PLACE DU CONSEIL DES QUINZE
R. Twinger
Bd J.-B. Bach
Allée de Robertsau
Bd Tauler
R. Massenet
Allée Richard Wagner
Rue d'Ypres
Quai Rouget de Lisle
Schweighauser
Rue Beethoven
Boulevard d'Anvers
Bd de la Marne
Rue de l'Yser
Rue de Rotterdam
Canal du Rhône au Rhin
PLACE GOLBERY
R. Geiler
Rue Wimpheling
PLACE ARNOLD
PLACE SÉBASTIEN BRANT
Avenue de la Forêt Noire
Rue d'Ostende
Rue Goethe
L'UNIVERSITÉ
Jardin botanique
R. de l'Observatoire
Bd Leblois
Rue de Louvain
Rue de l'Université
Place d'Islande
Rue du Grand Pont
PONT D'ANVERS
Boulevard de la Victoire
Université
Observatoire
Rue Vauban

GERMAN SHELLS FROM 1870

①

Discreet reminders of a terrible bombardment

8, rue du Gazon – 27, rue Sainte-Élisabeth – 7, rue du Vieux-Marché-aux-Poissons – 18, quai Saint-Nicolas – 9, quai des Pêcheurs – 1, rue d'Austerlitz – 12, place de la Cathédrale – 1, place du Temple Neuf – Musée historique, 2, rue du Vieux-Marché-aux-Poissons
Other shells can be found in the inner courtyard behind the restaurant Les Douze Apôtres, 7, rue Mercière (generally closed to the public, but sometimes accessible on request).

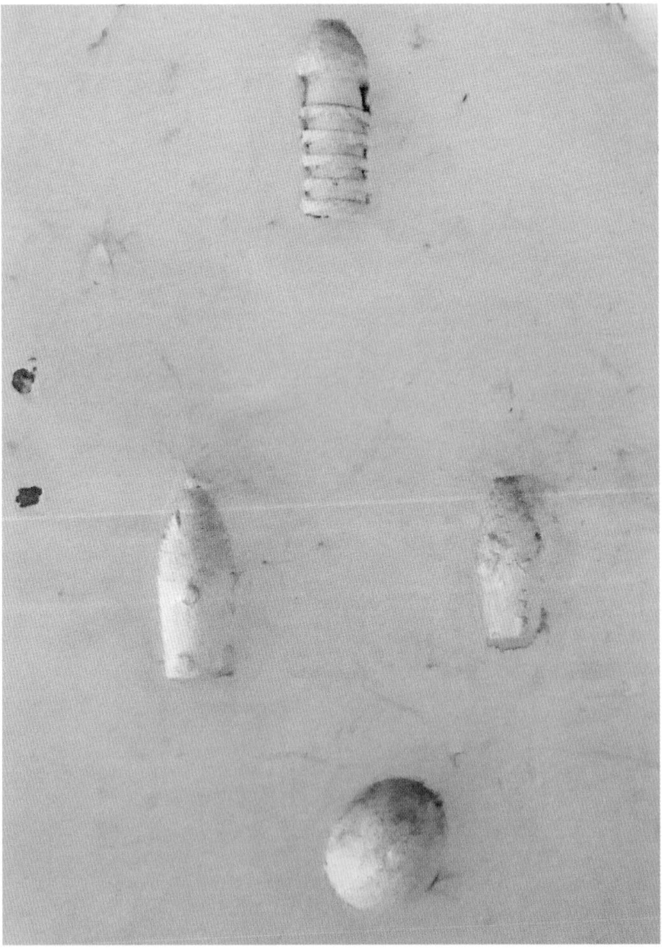

Few passers-by realise that several façades in Strasbourg still bear the scars of the Franco-German War of 1870: embedded in the stonework of certain buildings are actual German artillery shells, left in place for the sake of memory.

These relics mark the siege of Strasbourg, one of the war's most violent episodes. The conflict pitted France against a German coalition led by Prussia and joined by Bavaria, Württemberg, and the Grand Duchy of Baden – all part of the North German Confederation.

The French Empire surrendered on 10 May 1871, signing the Treaty of Frankfurt, which ceded Alsace-Lorraine to the German Reich, forever changing the region's fate.

But in order to achieve a French surrender German forces had to breach the defences of Strasbourg's fortress which, alongside Metz, was considered one of the strongest in France.

The siege of Strasbourg, commanded by Prussian General August von Werder, lasted from 16 August to 28 September 1870. On the night of 24 August, German shells destroyed the church of the Dominicans, dating from the 13th century, which housed a renowned library (including the medieval encyclopedia 'Hortus deliciarum' – 'Garden of Delights' – by the nun Herrad of Landsberg). The damage was so severe that no restoration was attempted. In its place a 'New Temple' was built, dedicated to Protestants but accessible to all. Planned from 1873, it was consecrated on 15 July 1888.

A monument commemorating the many victims of this conflict stands in the courtyard of the École Supérieure des Arts Décoratifs de Strasbourg (now part of Haute École des Arts du Rhin).

The siege of Strasbourg

An excerpt from the correspondence between Generals Werder (Germany) and Uhrich (France):

Werder: *'For two days, you have seen the damage I have done with only a portion of my artillery – to the city, its defences, and the fortress. At dawn, I shall cease fire to give you time to consider whether you now wish to surrender.'*

Réponse de Uhrich: *'My walls still stand, and I would not dream of surrendering a place that both the honour and the interest of France command me to defend to the bitter end.'*

GREEN MAN FROM THE BUILDING AT 1, RUE SELLÉNICK

②

Reminder of the importance of nature and the existence of "the spirit of the forest"

1, rue Sellénick
Viewing from outside only

At the corner of Rue Sellénick and Avenue des Vosges stand two Art Nouveau buildings, Nos. 1 and 3, rue Sellénick, designed between 1902 and 1904 by architects Franz Lükte and Heinrich Backes at the request of Bertha Wund and her husband Johann Moeller, advisor to the court of auditors.

Lükte himself took up residence in one of the apartments once the work was completed.

In 1905, Bertha Wund established the parent company of the tobacco business she managed on the ground floor of No. 3.

At the entrance to No. 1, note the wrought iron with plant-like motifs, overhanging the finely carved head of a man whose hair and beard cascade like foliage, spreading outwards along the top of the doorway.

This striking figure, a splendid example of a 'green man' (see following double-page spread), recalls the role of nature in Art Nouveau decoration (see p. 222).

Also at No. 1, the gable of the building features a graceful floral frieze.

A careful observer will notice that savings were made on materials: while the lower façades are built in ashlar stone, the upper floors are in plaster made to imitate it.

The green man

Whether on medieval façades or later Art Nouveau buildings, travellers across Europe may discover a curious figure if they look closely: a man whose head is crowned with foliage, sometimes with branches sprouting from his mouth.

Known as the 'green man', he symbolises the respect owed to nature – once dominated by humankind, now increasingly recognised as something to live in harmony with.

His meaning connects him to Silvanus, the Roman god of the forest, and to the spirit of the woods in shamanic traditions: an invisible but living force that must be honoured, under penalty of grave consequences.

The green man reminds us of the cycles of nature, renewed each spring, and embodies rebirth and new beginnings. His message is that nothing is permanent: even misfortunes that seem insurmountable eventually fade, and may in the long run be seen as trials that contribute to the soul's evolution.

The term itself was coined by Lady Raglan in her 1937 article 'The Green Man in Church Architecture' published in The Folklore Journal.

Three main types of green man can be distinguished: the leafy head, completely covered with foliage; the head with vegetation sprouting from the mouth; and the head with greenery bursting

from all the facial openings – nose, ears and mouth. The first type, which appeared mainly during the Renaissance and Baroque periods, generally resembles leafy masks with symmetrical vegetal patterns. The latter two, almost exclusively medieval, were intended to inspire awe and even fear, as representations of a forest king who demanded respectful conduct under threat of reprisal.
Although its origins lie in paganism, the motif became widespread on the capitals of Gothic churches and cathedrals, though it sometimes appears on secular buildings.
It enjoyed a revival in the late 19th and early 20th centuries and can be found throughout Europe, particularly in the UK, as well as in Thailand, India and Nepal.
In Anglo-Saxon folklore, the green man is often linked with another woodland spirit: Jack-in-the-Green.

SCULPTURE OF THE ALSATIAN ③

A little-known witness to the history of the press

Muller Simonis house
5, rue Saint-Léon
Bus H – Place de Pierre stop
Tram C – Place Broglie stop

At 5, rue Saint-Léon in the Neustadt district, an intriguing architectural detail catches the eye of curious passers-by: a sculpture of an Alsatian man seated on a pile of books. Perched on the third floor of the building, this picturesque figure was the emblem of Le Nouveau Alsacien (Der Elsässer), a bilingual Catholic daily newspaper founded in 1885, which remained a cornerstone of intellectual debate in Alsace for over a century until its closure in 1986.

The history of this building is closely tied to that of the regional press. Constructed between 1893 and 1895 by the architect Eugène Dacheux, it was commissioned by the priest and patron Paul Müller-Simonis, founder of the newspaper.

As industrial buildings were prohibited in this residential area, the print shop was discreetly installed in the courtyard at the back.

The eclectic architecture, with its French influences, features refined elements such as sculpted window frames and a mansard roof, reflecting the Parisian imprint on Strasbourg's late 19th-century urban design.

The statue of the Alsatian, created in 1894 by sculptor J. Huber, once sat above the entrance to the newspaper's offices, embodying the culture and identity of Alsace.

An outfit that makes sense

The figure is dressed in a buttoned vest, long-sleeved jacket, neck scarf and traditional culottes.

His bicorne (two-cornered) hat – an essential element of his attire – reflects the French influence on Alsatian men's fashion after the annexation of 1871. At a time when Alsace oscillated between French and German identities, this costume became a powerful symbol of regional belonging.

This emblem of respectability and seriousness was used in newspaper advertisements between the two world wars. Far more than mere decoration, the statue symbolised *Le Nouveau Alsacien*'s commitment to defending Alsatian particularism in an era of profound political and cultural upheaval.

'LA RACINE' SCULPTURES

④

A sculpture that hugs the shape of the rock

Garden of Palais du Rhin
1, place de la République
Tram B, C, E, F – République stop
Bus 15a, 72 – République stop

Given by the artist to the state and installed in the garden of the Palais du Rhin, the spectacular stone sculpture by René Hetzel, 'La Racine' (1952, 2.40 metres long), depicts a woman reclining lasciviously on a rock, her body embracing its contours.

The title 'La Racine' evokes a connection with the earth and nature: the sculpture forms an integral part of its environment, the woman's stretched posture suggesting both physical and symbolic rootedness, as if her body were part of the ground itself.

The influence of Aristide Maillol's early 20th-century sculpture is clear: Hetzel's full, softly modelled female forms echo those of Maillol.

The work conveys several essential themes: a reminder of humanity's link with the earth, as well as an allegory of femininity and fertility.

René Hetzel (1902–1972), a designer, engraver and sculptor, first drew attention in the art world during the 1925 Paris International Exhibition, when a series of his sculptures – including a central figure of a woman crouching after childbirth – sparked controversy.

© Roland Burckel

EFFIGIES OF EMPEROR WILHELM II

(5)

A nod to the new emperor of Reichsland Elsaß-Lothringen

Gates of the garden of the Palais du Rhin
Palais du Rhin
2, place de la République
The palace is open during the European Heritage Days.
The gates and railings are permanently visible from the outside

If one looks closely at the gates of the garden next to the Palais du Rhin, the wrought iron arabesques reveal an intriguing figure with a prominent moustache: this is the profile of Emperor Wilhelm II (1859–1941).

According to the Treaty of Frankfurt of 1871, Alsace and Moselle were annexed to the new German Empire. Strasbourg became the capital of Reichsland Elsaß-Lothringen.

When Emperor Wilhelm I of Hohenzollern (1797–1888) visited Strasbourg for the first time in 1877, he stayed at the Palais Klinglin (the present-day Hôtel du Préfet). Displeased with the residence, he ordered the construction of a new palace.

Built between 1883 and 1889 on the Kaiserplatz ('Emperor's Square,' now Place de la République), the palace was designed by Berlin architect Hermann Eggert (1844–1920). Its imposing architecture was meant to evoke imperial grandeur and embody 'the German spirit and the genius of its art,' as its creator put it.

This vast quadrilateral, spread across three levels, was adorned in a style combining the Italian (particularly Florentine) Renaissance and German Baroque.

At its centre stands a large audience chamber topped with a dome and fronted by a 'balcony of acclamations.' The emperor's private apartments, along with those of the empress, occupied the wings. The palace also contained formal reception halls, a grand function room, and a glazed courtyard. Outside were gardens and stables.

© Studio of Thomas Heinrich Voigt

It was conceived as an imperial residence fit to host foreign dignitaries and impress them with German power and ceremony.

The reception areas could accommodate 700 to 900 guests. No detail was overlooked: the profile of Wilhelm II – Wilhelm I's grandson – was even incorporated into the gates of the palace. It was Wilhelm II who officially inaugurated the building in August 1889.

POSTER ON THE FAÇADE OF THE ESCA

⑥

A little-known relic of the Liberation

28, avenue de la Marseillaise (to the left of nos 2–14, rue des Pontonniers)

While most people in Strasbourg are familiar with the grand building known as 'de l'ESCA' – the name of the provident society that commissioned its construction in the 1930s – very few notice a remarkable historical detail affixed to its façade.

Renowned for the quality of its apartments (it was the first residence in Strasbourg to offer as many garages as housing units), the building hides a small yet meaningful relic: a reproduction of a poster dated 16 April 1945, mounted at number 28 Avenue de la Marseillaise, shielded by a plexiglass frame.

Beneath the reproduction lies what remains of the original poster, glued directly onto the stone; some fragments were still visible as recently as 2011. The location of this relic is no accident.

During the Third Reich, the building was commandeered to serve as the seat of the regional constituency, under the authority of Gauleiter Robert Wagner (1895–1946).

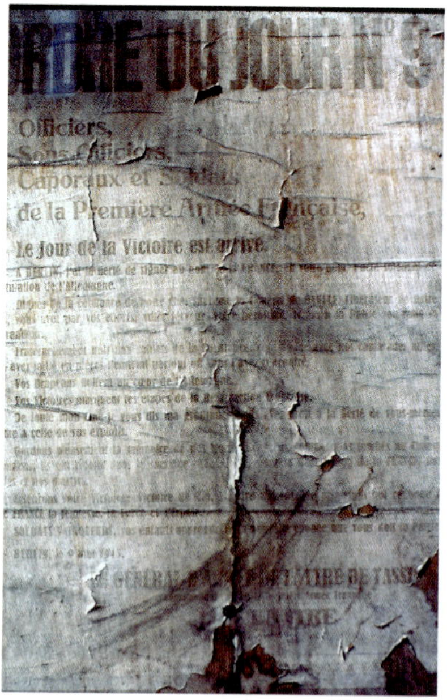

When Strasbourg was liberated by Leclerc's 2nd Armoured Division on 23 November 1944, the city's mayor, Charles Frey (1888–1955), announced the imminent arrival of General Jean de Lattre de Tassigny (1889–1952). To mark the occasion, a public ceremony was held in Place Broglie, featuring a military parade, a reception at City Hall, and a solemn celebration at the cathedral.

TEMPLE OF FRÉDÉRIC PITON

7

A hotspot for ongoing Speculative Masonry

Cercle philosophique Goethe
11, rue du Maréchal Joffre
Guided tours during the European Heritage Days

No. 11, rue du Maréchal Joffre, is a surprising building – not only for its perfectly maintained neo-Renaissance façade but also for its perpetually closed shutters. The site houses a discreet Masonic temple, one of the oldest in Strasbourg.

Few people know that it is possible to visit during the European Heritage Days, when guided tours are available.

This temple is named after Frédéric-Théodore Piton (1800–1871), a Strasbourg-born bookbinder, bookseller, publisher and librarian. Piton was also a Freemason and a member of the 'Frères Réunis.'

Speculative Freemasonry appeared in Strasbourg between 1743 and 1744. By the 18th century, three important lodges had been established: 'Saint-Jean d'Hérédom de Sainte-Geneviève,' 'le Parfait Silence' and 'Candeur.' A lodge is a meeting place for Freemasons.

At the beginning of the 19th century, Strasbourg was home to six lodges. The one to which Piton belonged ('Frères Réunis') merged with two others in 1841, 'les Cœurs Fidèles' and 'la Vraie Fraternité.' It became a highly influential lodge, encouraging charitable works and the creation of public schools. One of its most famous members, Jean-François Macé (1815–1894 – a teacher, journalist and politician of working-class origins – was among the founders of the Ligue de l'Enseignement in 1866.

With this influence, the 'Frères Réunis' sought to foster closer relations between French and German lodges by inaugurating a statue of Erwin, the reputed master-builder of Notre-Dame Cathedral (see p. 140), in Steinbach, Germany – Erwin's supposed birthplace. However, after the Franco-Prussian War, the French lodges were replaced in 1872 by German lodges affiliated with the Grand Lodge of Prussia.

Today, the Grand Orient de France has resumed its activities in the Piton Temple, now home to the Cercle philosophique Goethe. The building houses six Obediences, several lodges and two temples, including the one on the first floor, which was listed as a Historic Monument in 1993.

BUILDING AT 14, RUE DU GÉNÉRAL GOURAUD

8

Artistic and political allegory

14, rue du Général Gouraud
Viewing from outside only

Built between 1902 and 1903 by architect Samuel Landshut, this beautiful Art Nouveau building stands at the corner of Avenue des Vosges and Rue du Général Gouraud.

On completion, it became both his main residence and his architecture studio.

Particularly striking are the two mosaics of women's faces on the first floor, placed on either side of the corner façade.

One, with closed eyes, personifies Night; the other, with blue eyes, represents Day. Both are crowned with flowers in the Art Nouveau style (see following double-page spread).

Above the two heads sits the German imperial eagle in the Jugendstil tradition, a more geometric form of Art Nouveau rooted in Germany.

Today, the building is private property, divided into apartments.

Art Nouveau in Strasbourg

Strasbourg, located almost equidistant between Nancy and Darmstadt – two of the leading centres of French and German Art Nouveau – was itself an important hub of the movement between 1895 and 1914.

Architectural activity flourished particularly in the Neustadt, a district created under the 1880 urban plan that tripled the city's size when Strasbourg was capital of Reichsland Elsass-Lothringen.

Around 70 to 80 Art Nouveau buildings remain, representing roughly 10% of the constructions from the German administration.

A first local manifesto was the École des Arts Décoratifs, founded in 1889 by Anton Seder, which introduced polychrome ceramics and plant-themed panels on façades.

The school became a training ground for crafters and artists, including leading architects such as Jules Berninger and Gustave Krafft, creators of Villa Schützenberger* (see p. 242).

Art Nouveau

The term 'Art Nouveau' was coined by the Hamburg-born art dealer Samuel Bing (1838–1905), who opened a gallery of that name in Paris in 1895.

There he showcased the work of many artists who would later become leading representatives of this new style, which quickly spread across Europe, taking on different local names.

In Germany and Austria, it became known as *Jugendstil* (Youth Style). The name derives from Die Jugend, a satirical weekly launched in Munich in 1896 by publisher Georg Hirth. His provocative approach and distinctive typography soon became associated with the artistic innovations of the time, giving rise to Jugendstil.

Other terms were also adopted in Europe.

In Austria, *Sezessionstil* referred to the Vienna Secession movement, founded by the symbolist painter Gustav Klimt in 1897.

In England, 'Liberty Style' took its name from the Liberty & Co boutique, renowned for its modern fabrics. 'Modern Style' came to encompass the two dominant European trends.

Popular nicknames, such as 'nouille' or 'spaghetti' style, also described the same aesthetic.

More than a straightforward artistic movement, Art Nouveau aspired to be a new way of thinking and living, rejecting the prevailing social model.

Breaking with eclecticism and mass production, it called for a union of art and craftsmanship, drawing direct inspiration from nature – sinuous plants, curves, and organic forms – and expressed itself in both the decorative arts and architecture.

Its ambition was to liberate society from the exploitation of the working class, the dominance of the Church, and restrictive notions of femininity.

This newfound sensuality and eroticism found expression in the numerous stylised depictions of women's heads that adorn the façades of Art Nouveau buildings.

The movement reached its peak between the late 19th century and 1914 but suffered a decline after the First World War.

With the urgent need for large-scale, low-cost reconstruction, Art Nouveau architecture could no longer meet the demands of the time.

BLUEPRINT OF THE ERUV IN STRASBOURG

9

A central element of the religious life of the Strasbourg Jews

Grande synagogue de la Paix
Avenue de la Paix
For information, contact the Consistoire israélite du Bas-Rhin:
1a, rue René Hirschler
03 88 14 46 50
cibr@cibr.fr

With the exception of members of Strasbourg's Orthodox Jewish community, few people know that the city has a ritual enclosure called the *eruv*, which plays a particularly important role during the Sabbath and certain festivals (see following pages).

The eruv in Strasbourg – whose blueprint is pinned to a panel at the entrance of the Grande Synagogue de la Paix, the seat of the Jewish community and the Chief Rabbinate of the Lower Rhine – is based on a Hebrew tradition with biblical roots. According to the traditional interpretation of two passages from Exodus (Ex. 16:29 and 36:6), during the Sabbath (Saturday) and Yom Kippur, it is forbidden to transport anything between private and public spaces for distances over two metres (see following double-page spread for more details).

Taken literally, this prohibition is highly restrictive: one cannot carry glasses in a pocket (though wearing them is permitted), nor carry keys, books, or heavier objects. To work around this, Strasbourg's Jewish community signed an agreement with the city designating certain public areas – made up of connected private properties – as being 'private' and under communal ownership. Within this enclosed zone – the eruv – transport is permitted, as it is no longer considered to cross into public space.

Depending on local topography, an eruv can be delineated using natural or artificial structures. In Israel or New York, for example, nylon wires are stretched between lampposts or street furniture. In Amsterdam, temporary chains were once used on Sabbaths and festival days to complete the enclosures formed by canals.

Strasbourg's layout lends itself well to an eruv: much of the city is encircled by watercourses whose banks act as natural fences. Another part of the enclosure follows the railway line toward Kehl. However, Orthodox Jews must ensure these rivers don't freeze in winter, as this would make them passable and break the enclosure.

The renown of Strasbourg's eruv continues to attract many Orthodox Jewish families who choose to settle within its boundaries.

For more information on Eruv and the Sabbath, see following double-page spread.

What is an Eruv?

The *eruv* or *eruv* (plural: *eruvin* or *eruvim*) is a symbolic enclosure set up by an Orthodox Jewish community. The point is to define a space in which certain otherwise prohibited activities (see opposite) can be carried out on the Sabbath (see opposite) and certain religious holidays.

By symbolically transforming public into private space, the eruv allows people to lead an almost normal life outside the home on those days.

Some things are allowed that under Sabbath rules would be restricted: leaving the house with keys in hand, using a walking stick, or carrying a child in your arms.

Originally, the boundaries of the eruvim coincided with those of the city walls, whose gates marked the transition from public to private property.

However, with the expansion of modern cities, this system became impractical.

New means have thus been implemented to enclose the ritual space depending on the configuration of the site: ropes, chains, or stretched threads replace the walls of the past. In Strasbourg, the greatest part of the eruv is enclosed by the watercourses of the city (see previous double page spread).

The Eruv of the City of Strasbourg

Strasbourg's eruv is the largest in France (others exist in Metz and Reims) and one of the largest in Europe.

Another notable eruv exists in Venice, which also gave the world the word 'ghetto' (see 'Secret Venice' also published by Jonglez).

The Sabbath

The Sabbath (*shabbat*) refers to Saturday, the seventh day of the week in Jewish tradition. Ritually the Sabbath extends from Friday sunset to Saturday evening, after the appearance of the first two stars.

The 39 activities that are prohibited during the Sabbath

On the Sabbath and some festivals, the Talmud forbids 39 types of activity, which are believed to relate to the building of the Tabernacle (the mobile sanctuary that housed the Ark of the Covenant).

These prohibitions therefore apply to actions that 'create' anything, or 'take control' of an entity outside the family sphere. The forbidden tasks include all the stages of breadmaking (planting, ploughing, harvesting, binding sheaves, threshing, winnowing, selecting, grinding, sifting, kneading, baking), textile production (shearing, bleaching, carding, dyeing, spinning, chain stitching, warping, weaving, unravelling, tying, untying, sewing, tearing), and leatherworking (trapping, slaughtering, skinning, tanning, smoothing, scraping, cutting).

It is also forbidden to write or erase more than two letters, or to build or demolish anything.

Fires must not be lit or extinguished, and in general, no task should be completed. The final prohibition concerns 'carrying – moving an object from a private domain to a public one.

WHITE ARROWS ON RUE CHARLES GRAD

Vestiges of a war-time signage system

5, rue Charles Grad

⑩

Several buildings in Strasbourg – including number 5, rue Charles Grad – still bear faint white painted arrows on their façades, which today go largely unnoticed.

Civil defence in Strasbourg dates back to the 1870s, long before the term itself came into use.

Having suffered bombardments during the Franco-Prussian War, and later in both world wars, the city began considering the protection of its civilian population very early on.

By 1935, still marked by the traumas of earlier conflicts, the city implemented formal measures to protect civilians.

This included organising the distribution of gas masks in the event of an attack, and building shelters (mainly in private or public cellars) to offer refuge during air raids.

To indicate these shelters – now mostly forgotten, though many still exist – Strasbourg developed a signage system that included these white arrows.

In case a building collapsed, designated evacuation passages were also established. Fire hydrants were marked with a capital 'H' (for 'hydrant').

Other phosphorescent arrows

In addition to these, white phosphorescent arrows (visible at night) were painted on the corners of buildings and on tree trunks. These belonged to a separate signage system introduced by the German authorities after annexation. The German-era arrows were displayed differently but always indicated the direction from the basement window towards the designated cellar shelter.

One remarkable remnant of this system is a former underground military hospital, built in 1937 beneath the car park of the Halles bus station. This secret, circular shelter covered 490 square metres and could accommodate up to 200 people. It is not open to the public and remains shrouded in secrecy, but records confirm that it was occupied by German civil defence forces following the annexation.

LEAKTEL BUILDING FAÇADE

⑪

Subtle marriage between neo-Renaissance and Art Nouveau

14, rue Charles Grad
Viewing from outside only

© Phil Lewis

Built between 1905 and 1906 for Martin Nebutel, senior manager of the Post Office, the imposing building at 14, rue Charles Grad was designed by architect Aloys Walter and completed by contractor Rudolf Stecher.

At first glance, its ashlar façade reflects a neo-Renaissance style, yet the abundant Art Nouveau decoration gives it particular distinction.

On the second-floor oriel, a striking male head emerges from foliage, adding an elegant and poetic touch above a graceful semi-circular window.

Above the first-floor windows are three remarkable sculpted reliefs: to the left, a woman's head in pure Art Nouveau style; to the right, an elderly man holding his beard in his hands alongside a chain; and a woman with a lyre.

Each figure is framed by finely carved trees, while delicately rendered vines extend above them (note, in particular, the veins visible on the old man's hands).

The entrance, deliberately set to the left, still bears the date '1905'.

On the fourth floor, a curious frieze of pretzels and flowers can be seen. On the ground floor, above the central windows, a cherub holds a heraldic crest with no inscription.

Renovated in 2013, the building is now divided into private apartments.

© Phil Lewis

VILLA KNOPF GATEWAY

⑫

Peacock wheel and butterfly, symbols of personal transformation

10, rue Schiller
Viewing from outside only

On the corner of Rue Schiller and Quai Rouget-de-Lisle, Villa Knopf boasts an exceptional Art Nouveau gateway.

Built between 1904 and 1905 for Moritz Knopf, owner of the city's department stores, the villa and its gateway were designed by architects Gustave Krafft and Jules Berninger, leading figures of Strasbourg's Art Nouveau movement.

At the centre of the enclosure, the wrought-iron gate unfolds in sweeping volutes and arabesques, poetically recalling the tail feathers of a peacock. Because it sheds its plumage in winter and regains it in spring, the peacock has long been regarded as a symbol of renewal and rebirth.

Beneath what resembles the peacock's wheel, the gateway itself takes the form of a butterfly poised to take flight.

Like the peacock, the butterfly is rich in symbolism. Its metamorphosis from egg to larva, cocoon to winged form, evokes change, transformation, and the courage to embrace evolution in order to soar.

Since 1996, the villa has belonged to the University of Strasbourg and today houses the Institute of Higher European Studies.

NEARBY

'La Création du Monde' fresco (13)

5, Place de Bordeaux (now the seat of France 3 Alsace)

From Place de Bordeaux, the glazed façade of the auditorium of the 'Nouvelle Maison de la Radio' (1956) allows a view of the vast ceramic work 'La Création du Monde', one of the favourite themes of its designer, Jean Lurçat. The fresco was created in 1961 by the ceramist Gumersind Gomila (1905–1970). Since it is only visible from a distance, behind glass, the work remains little known to Strasbourg residents. It depicts God's creation of the world in six days, according to Genesis, and reads from left to right: the creation of Heaven and Earth; the separation of Light and Darkness; of Water and Land; of Light (the Moon and the Sun); the creation of plants, fish, birds and animals. Finally, in accordance with the Biblical account, Man dominates the entire system: placed above the other representations, he appears in the form of a head made of red flames. The fresco was listed as a Historic Monument in 1983.

THE LIBRARY OF THE VILLA HERRENSCHMIDT

14

A spectacular library of Alsatics

4, rue Raiffeisen
First floor
03 88 14 72 55
bacm.creditmutuel.fr
Wednesday to Friday : 9am–12pm and 1pm–4.30pm (booking required)
On-site consultation only
Tram line B – Wacken (direction Hoenheim Gare)

On the first floor of the Villa Herrenschmidt, now owned by Crédit Mutuel, sits one of Strasbourg's most exceptional libraries. It holds approximately 41,000 volumes, the majority of which are categorised as Alsatics – literary or scientific works related to the Alsace region.

Alsatics are a distinct cultural feature of France, continuing a centuries-old tradition of regional scholarship.

In the 19th century, the building was the residence of Charles Schulmeister, a spy for Emperor Napoleon I, before becoming the property of the Herrenschmidt family, a prominent dynasty of tanners.

Due to hygiene and odour concerns, tanning could no longer be carried out in the city centre.

The Wacken district, situated at Strasbourg's edge and irrigated by the River Aar, became the ideal place to continue these activities, which lasted into the 20th century.

The library owes its rare and valuable collection to Antoine Gardner, a passionate bibliophile who inherited the books in 1972.

In the 1980s, the collection was moved to Crédit Mutuel's headquarters at 34, rue du Wacken. In 1998, it was transferred to the restored first floor of Villa Herrenschmidt, where it remains today.

A moving façade

In 1924, after learning that the façade of the former Banque de France on Place Broglie was to be dismantled, Georges Herrenschmidt purchased the neoclassical stones. He had them reassembled and grafted onto his villa's façade in Wacken.

This is why the caduceus of Mercury, symbolising trade and finance, still adorns the building's entrance gate – a unique nod to both banking and family legacy.

'LE PUITS VOLEUR' INSTALLATION ⑮

Journey to the Moon

Parc de l'Orangerie
Bus 30, C6 – Conseil de l'Europe stop

In the heart of Strasbourg's Parc de l'Orangerie, 'Le Puits Voleur' ('The Thieving Well') by Patrick Bailly-Maître-Grand is often overlooked

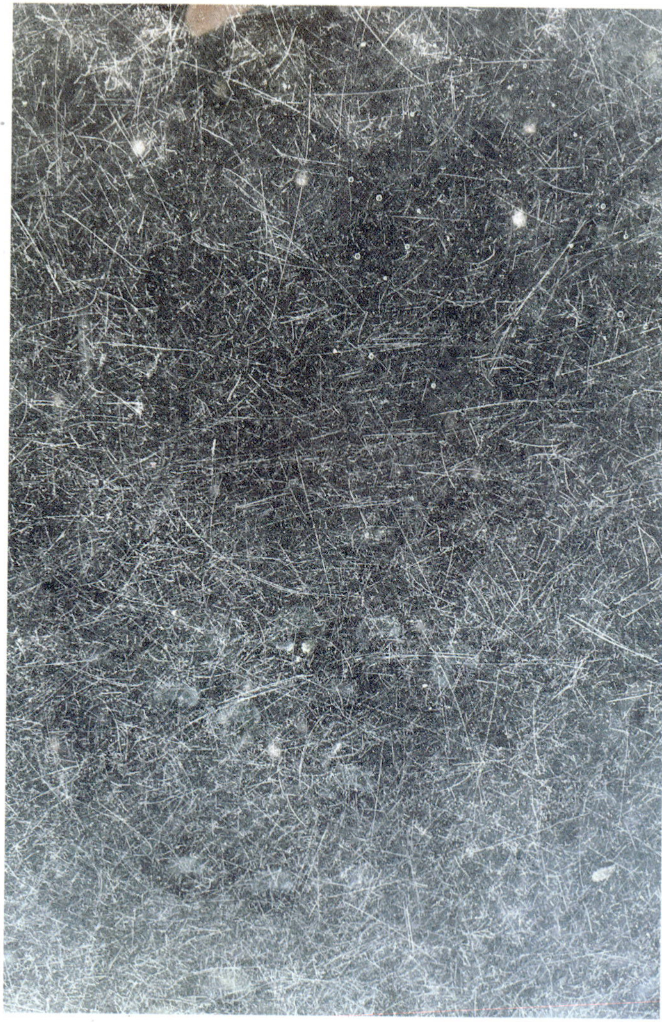

by passers-by. From a distance, the installation appears intriguing: four pillars support a dome, reminiscent of a small temple or observatory. Up close, visitors discover a celestial vault dotted with 500 stars, seemingly suspended in weightlessness. But the true surprise lies at the bottom of the well, where a glowing full moon awaits.

The well contains no water but rather an illusion: what visitors believe they see is merely a reflection – an image trapped in the artist's optical device. Bailly-Maître-Grand here plays with mirrors and light, creating a disconcerting trompe-l'œil that condenses the universe and brings it within reach.

Lowering your gaze produces the uncanny sensation of approaching the Moon in reverse perspective, as though reliving Galileo's discovery of its contours for the first time.

Discreet and little known, this work reveals itself gradually. Neither monumental nor spectacular, it invites visitors to slow down and search for the hidden. A well-kept secret – a doorway to a fragment of the universe, concealed within the park. An invitation to contemplate and dream.

BUEREHIESEL RESTAURANT BUILDING ⑯

A rare and little-known vestige of the 1895 exhibition

4, parc de l'Orangerie
Park opens every day 7am–8pm – Restaurant open Tuesday afternoon to Saturday evening, 12pm–1.30pm and 7.30pm–9pm

© Fabien Romary

The Buerehiesel ('peasants' house') in Parc de l'Orangerie is today better known for its fine cuisine than for its forgotten history. Originally a grocery shop in an old Alsatian farmhouse built in 1607 in downtown Molsheim, it was dismantled, transported and rebuilt here, piece by piece, for the industrial and craft exhibition of 1895 (see following double-page spread), complete with a vegetable garden and gazebo. It is one of only two surviving structures from that exhibition (see p. 294).

In 1894, city architect Johann-Karl Ott, assisted by Édouard Roederer of the municipal services, drew up plans for the reassembly. While preserving the generous carved Renaissance framework, he also drew inspiration from the farms of Kaysersberg and Riquewihr.

One small detail: when the house was reassembled a year later, the little oriel was mounted in reverse and now hangs on the right corner of the main façade.

Listed as a historical monument in 1979 for its authentic framework and joinery, the Buerehiesel has survived many hazards.

Threatened with demolition during the Second World War, it was saved thanks to the intervention of the Conservator of Historic Monuments, who underlined its heritage value.

In 1989, a glass roof designed by Guy Walter was added to protect the terrace, and in 2003 the original frescoes depicting Alsatian rural scenes were rediscovered and restored.

Converted into a restaurant, it was taken over in 1970 by Antoine Westermann, who won his first Michelin star here in 1976.

Exposition Industrielle et Artisanale of 1895 in Strasbourg: a showcase of regional know-how

With the Industrial Revolution and the growing international outlook of the 19th and early 20th centuries, entrepreneurs sought to display their expertise and inventions while conquering new markets.

This gave rise to the vogue for universal exhibitions, combining commercial rivalry with national pride. Strasbourg was no exception, and from 1895 onwards it hosted major thematic events. To promote the know-how of the Reichsland ('Territory of the Empire', the German name for Alsace-Lorraine when annexed by the German Empire between 1871 and 1918), Strasbourg inaugurated the Industrial and Craft Exhibition on 15 May 1895 in the districts of Baden, the Palatinate and Hesse.

The exhibition, which ran until October in the Orangerie Park, was seen as a local response to World Fairs, blending technical demonstrations, commercial competition and the showcasing of regional heritage.

To host more than 1,200 exhibitors, the eastern half of the park was completely redesigned in the style of an English garden. A large lake with two basins was dug, a cave-waterfall constructed, and winding avenues bordered with greenhouses and ornate parterres were laid out.

Around this landscaped setting rose vast wooden halls displaying metalwork, textiles, ceramics and decorative arts, while the Pavillon Joséphine provided an exhibition space for masterpieces of local heritage.

Among the rare permanent buildings were two notable examples: the Molsheim 'peasant house', dismantled in 1894 and rebuilt stone by stone on the lake shore (see previous double-page spread), and the administrative building, later moved to 102 Route de Schirmeck to house the restaurant Au Nid de Cigognes (see p. 294).

Beyond its popular success, the 1895 Exhibition had a lasting impact on Strasbourg's urban planning. The redevelopment of the Orangerie marked the park's integration into the Neustadt (new town) and stimulated the creation of new avenues.

It also provided a model for later large-scale exhibitions: the annual itinerant German agricultural fair at the Meinau (1913), followed by the major events held at Wacken between the two world wars. These included a patriotic exhibition celebrating the return of Alsace to France (1919) and a commemoration of the centenary of

Pasteur's birth (1923).
For the latter, part of the Wacken land allocated to the city of Ungemach was converted into an exhibition park.
In 1924, these halls and wooden pavilions hosted the grand exhibition in honour of the French colonial empire. Two years later, the Wacken site became the venue for an annual autumn fair, the forerunner of today's European Fair.
During the 1930s, the temporary wooden halls were gradually replaced by solid, modernist buildings.
In 1935 a new exhibition dedicated to hygiene was held, and throughout the decade a wide range of other events took place across the city.

VILLA SCHÜTZENBERGER FAÇADE

17

Art Nouveau Strasbourg style

76, allée de la Robertsau
Viewing from outside only

Villa Schützenberger, at 76, allée de la Robertsau, is a sumptuous Art Nouveau residence (see p. 222) built between 1898 and 1900 by the architects Gustave Krafft and Jules Berninger.

The house was commissioned by Louis Oscar Schützenberger, heir to the renowned Schützenberger family brewery in Schiltigheim.

Note the monumental wrought-iron gate, façades decorated with

© Patrick

sculpted floral bouquets, and finely crafted ironwork, where the arum (a flower symbolising burning desire) is entwined with other plant motifs.

Inspired by Italian, particularly Tuscan, villas, the residence is arranged on two levels, with two wings set at an angle.

Despite its elegance, the villa nearly disappeared in 1972 to make way for an apartment complex.

It was saved thanks to the mobilisation of heritage campaigners and was listed in the Inventaire Supplémentaire des Monuments Historiques in 1975.

Since 1989, Villa Schützenberger has hosted many European events. Its ground and lower floors are home to the Association Parlementaire Européenne and the Observatoire Européen de l'Audiovisuel.

CROMER BUILDING FAÇADE

18

A discreet Art Nouveau jewel

56, allée de la Robertsau
Viewing from outside only

Not far from Villa Schützenberger, the Cromer building is another of Strasbourg's discreet yet magnificent examples of Art Nouveau. Look up to admire the ceramic panels on the top two floors, inspired by Otto Wagner's 1898 Majolikahaus (Majolica House) in Vienna. Here, the panels elegantly depict white lily flowers with red and green foliage against a blue background.

At each end of the façade is a curious rounded gable, openwork on the sides.

In the centre, beneath the balcony set below the ceramic panels, intertwined branches and baskets of fruit frame four faces that seem submerged in vegetation.

These discreet figures are examples of the so-called 'green men' (see p. 210), symbols of respect for nature.

The two lateral oriels feature floral garlands ending in lion's paws, topped with decorations shaped like elephant tusks.

On the ground floor, the central columns are particularly striking, their capitals carved into an extraordinary tangle of branches and leaves.

The building was constructed between 1902 and 1904 by Franz Lütke and Heinrich Backes for George Cromer, a master baker from Robertsau.

Influenced by the Darmstadt School (one of the principal centres of German Jugendstil), the architects distanced themselves from the flamboyant arabesques of French Art Nouveau.

Instead, they opted for a straighter geometry, which was perceived at the time as a welcome renewal in contrast to curved lines considered overly romantic.

Listed on the Inventaire Supplémentaire des Monuments Historiques since 1975, the building is today private property, divided into several apartments.

© Phil Lewis

HÔTEL BRION FAÇADE

⑲

One of the most beautiful Art Nouveau achievements in Strasbourg

22, rue Sleidan
Viewing from outside only

A few steps from the botanical garden stands Hôtel Brion, one of Strasbourg's most beautiful examples of Art Nouveau architecture.

Its elegant ashlar façade features a magnificent portal with delicately curved lines and a wrought-iron fence reminiscent of dragonfly wings – a motif, like the peacock and butterfly (see p. 233), symbolising transformation and evolution.

Above the entrance, note the stained-glass window in the shape of a heart, a form repeated at the base of the door.

The house was built between 1904 and 1905 by architect Auguste Brion (1861–1940) for his own use, but in 1908 it was bought by Carl Wirtz, who later added a winter garden.

As a result, Brion – who owned the property for only three years – never actually lived there.

In 1929 Wirtz converted the residence into a boarding house under the name Hôtel Marguerite, accommodating travellers and merchants until he abruptly ended the venture.

The building was listed in the Inventaire Supplémentaire des Monuments Historiques in 1975 for its façade, roof and spectacular entrance gate.

Today Hôtel Brion is privately owned and can only be admired from the street.

‘MÉDITATIONS’ SCULPTURE

20

A very special sundial

Gardens of Palais Universitaire
Tram C – Université stop – Gallia stop

At the heart of the gardens of Strasbourg's Palais Universitaire stands 'Méditations', a 1996 installation by Mac Adams that, surprisingly, attracts little attention despite being in a busy, well-used space.

Designed in aluminium and pebbles from Delaware (USA), the sculpture stretches over three metres and integrates harmoniously into its environment, inviting both aesthetic and philosophical contemplation.

At first glance, the piece resembles an abstract structure: a metallic rod surmounted by two trays holding pebbles, like a strange metallic flower.

But 'Méditations' is much more than a simple sculpture. It is a monumental sundial, whose projected shadow only reveals its true meaning at certain times of the year. From May to July, between midday and 1.30 pm, the shadow of the structure gradually transforms into the silhouette of a man seated in the lotus position, deep in meditation.

Mac Adams plays with light and time, making his work ephemeral and ever-changing. 'When it doesn't work, this sculpture exists as a silent transmitter, an abstract form, and the shadow's silhouette is present only as a memorised image,' explains the artist.

Beyond its technical ingenuity, 'Méditations' encourages passers-by to slow down and observe nature. The movement of the shadow, punctuated by the movement of the Sun, invites a contemplative pause – a sensory and spiritual experience.

SWASTIKA AT THE PALAIS UNIVERSITAIRE OF STRASBOURG

(21)

A symbol dating from well before the Nazis

9, place de l'Université
Tram C, F – Université stop – Gallia stop

Few students at the Palais Universitaire of Strasbourg notice the frieze running along the steps of the inner courtyard, particularly on the west side. It features black-and-white mosaics with alternating squares, each marked by a black dot in the centre. Among these is a symbol often seen yet frequently misunderstood: the swastika, an ancient emblem of life and regeneration used for thousands of years.

This swastika dates from the construction of the university campus in 1884, when Strasbourg was part of the Reichsland Elsass-Lothringen (Imperial Territory of Alsace-Lorraine, under German rule from 1871 to 1918).

It therefore bears no connection to the Nazis, who came to power only in the 1930s.

Authentic Nazi swastikas at Palais Universitaire

Ironically, while this swastika has no Nazi associations, the inner courtyard did feature genuine Nazi symbols during the annexation of Alsace (1940–44).

The university was occupied by the authorities of the Third Reich, who placed swastikas on the paving of the courtyard, at the south-eastern and north-eastern ends.

These were erased after the war, though only superficially: the paving was altered on two arms of the swastikas to render them unrecognisable.

With a careful eye, however, it is still possible to imagine how they once looked.

'ARGENTORATA' AND 'GERMANIA' STATUES ㉒

A symbol of the new Franco-German friendship

Palais Universitaire
9, place de l'Université
Tram C, E or F – Gallia – Université – Observatoire
Bus 10 or 30 – Gallia

In September 2014, two long-lost statues were finally restored to the façade of the Palais Universitaire in celebration of its 130th anniversary.

Thanks to archival photographs, a generous sponsor, and a modern spirit of Franco-German reconciliation – especially after the Élysée Treaty of 1963 – sculptors recreated the allegorical figures Germania and Argentorata (Latin for Strasbourg) in Burgundy limestone.

Inaugurated in 1884 by Emperor Wilhelm I of Prussia, the building's neo-Renaissance façade was intended to show neighbouring France the excellence of teaching in the German Empire.

Beneath the inscription *Litteris and Patriae* (To Letters and the Fatherland), it featured statues of allegories of Germany ('Germania') and Strasbourg ('Argentorata', *Argentoratum* being the Latin name of the city).

The First World War, however, got the better of the 'Germania' statue. French academics, driven by strong nationalist sentiments (some libraries even stopped ordering books and journals written in German for years), French academics couldn't stand the presence of this personification of the enemy. In 1919 students beheaded and then smashed the statue.

As for 'Argentorata', it only outlived Germania for about 30 years. Nazi Germany, which seized the city in 1940, destroyed the second statue in revenge.

For decades the two niches were left empty, which many Strasbourgeois thought was just the whim of an architect. Their reinstatement in 2014 was a powerful symbol of European unity.

'LA RIVIÈRE SOUTERRAINE' ARTWORK

23

A jewel hidden in street furniture

Intersection of Boulevard de la Marne and Boulevard d'Anvers
Tram C, E – Observatoire stop
Bus 2 – Saint Maurice stop

Installed in 2008 at the intersection of Boulevard de la Marne and Boulevard d'Anvers, on both sides of the road, 'La Rivière Souterraine' (The Underground River) by Jean-Luc Moulène is a particularly discreet artwork, resembling a security fence at first glance.

Both functional and poetic, this installation in painted galvanised steel is part of the Route de l'Art Contemporain (see below).

The work unfolds in sinuous lines that evoke creeping vines, its undulating forms contrasting with the rigidity of traditional urban structures. Inspired by biomorphism, it plays on the tension between the solidity of steel and the fluidity of the design.

The title is not merely a poetic image: a real water pipe (channelled from the Mühlwasser river), a relic of the city's former hydraulic system, lies beneath this crossroads.

Route de l'Art Contemporain

Strasbourg's Route of Contemporary Art is an open-air artistic journey, created between 1990 and 2000 to showcase contemporary art in public spaces. Transforming the city into a true open-air museum, it brings together a series of permanent works installed across the different neighbourhoods, freely accessible to all, 24 hours a day, seven days a week.

The project reflects a desire to make art part of daily urban life, integrated into architecture, squares, crossroads, parks and public buildings. Its goals are to democratise access to art by taking it out of museums and placing it within the urban landscape, to encourage dialogue between artworks, residents and the environment, to support contemporary creativity and to establish Strasbourg as a genuine hub of artistic experimentation.

The project is run by the City of Strasbourg in conjunction with the Centre Européen d'Actions Artistiques Contemporaines (CEAAC).

The works are extremely varied: sculptures, installations, subtle interventions, hybrid objects and more.

ROHRSCHOLLEN ISLAND

24

A nature reserve hidden in an industrial zone

Take the N353 (south ring road) towards Offenburg. Before crossing the Rhine at the Pfimlin bridge, exit at 'Port de Strasbourg', then follow signs to 'Usine d'incinération'. Continue past the hydroelectric plant, then take the right-hand fork (asphalt road) to the car park.
Free guided tours available
Book at: rn-rohrschollen.strasbourg.eu

Largely unknown to most of Strasbourg's residents, the island of Rohrschollen is hidden in plain sight. Nestled in the city's industrial port zone, it lies between a waste incineration facility and a hydroelectric power plant – hardly a place one expects to find a haven of nature.

And yet, this partially manmade island, landscaped in 1970, has become a vital stopover for migratory birds. Some 158 species are recorded in summer, and around 4,000 waterbirds winter here annually.

Covering 309 hectares, the Rohrschollen reserve is a sanctuary for insects, especially dragonflies and praying mantises. Its meadows and alluvial forests offer a rare glimpse of the Rhine's natural landscape before modern industry.

The island's name is rooted in that past : 'Schollen' were mounds of earth emerging during seasonal flooding, on which 'Rohr' (hollow reeds) grew. Today's island, bordered by the canalised Rhine to the west and the Old Rhine to the east, remains flood-prone.

A stream called the Bauerngrundwasser, fed by the water table, flows freely across the land – splitting the island in two. Over time, its winding course has created ponds and wetlands.

This flourishing environment has also reclaimed wartime ruins: many blockhouses built during the Second World War remain, now covered in thick alluvial vines, creepers, hops and wild clematis.

To explore the reserve, visitors can choose from three walking trails developed by the City of Strasbourg:

Oie Cendrée, Vieux Rhin, and Forêt Galerie – all offering stops for birdwatching and views of this remarkable ecosystem, which was declared a National Nature Reserve in 1997.

Strasbourg Port du Rhin'Post Office: the former harbour master's office at the Port du Rhin

Few people in Strasbourg realise that the imposing building currently housing the Strasbourg Port du Rhin post office once served as the harbour master's office (see opposite).

This neo-historicist building stood on what was known as the Île-aux-Épis (Island of Spikes), named after the *épis*, retention and stabilization spikes that once separated Strasbourg from the Rhine: this was the name given to the submerged masonry structures, perpendicular to the current, which reduced the flow of the river.

Built at the end of the 19th century, these *groynes* reduced the river's current where the canalization of the Rhine made navigation difficult: unable to spread out, the river picked up speed and, without the action of these *groynes*, could not be navigated by boats.

The harbour master's office once served as the command centre of the port, at a time when the area was crowded daily with barges carrying coal, grain, timber, foodstuffs and everyday goods.

The building's imposing appearance underscored its administrative importance.

Constructed in 1899 by architect Gustave-Adolphe Oberthur (1872–1965), the grey sandstone building is inspired by medieval and Renaissance architecture.

Its stepped gables, oriels and decorative friezes give it a unique character, reminiscent of the Petites Boucheries on Rue de la Haute Montée – another of Oberthur's creations.

The Port du Rhin : a port that moved three times

Strasbourg occupies an almost central position in the natural corridor of the Upper Rhine valley linking Basel to Mainz.

On the southern side, the Saône and Rhône valleys (the canal from Saône to Rhine was completed in 1832, and from Rhône to Rhine in 1834), opened the route to Mediterranean Europe; to the north, it provided access to the great plains of northern Europe. Since at least the Middle Ages, Strasbourg was also an essential stop for the river trade between Flanders and northern Italy, despite frequent flooding and the instability of the Rhine riverbed, which persisted until the ambitious development work of the 19th century. But the importance of Strasbourg in Rhine river traffic was obvious from 1331 with the founding of the Ancre corporation, which brought the city's mariners together and monopolised the transport of people and goods on the Rhine between Strasbourg and Mainz. Until the end of the 19th century the port was still on the banks of the Ill, not far from the Ancienne Douane (Old Customs, built in 1358). But the constraints of industrialisation meant relocation – three times. In 1882 the excavation of the Umleitungskanal (diversion channel) connecting the Marne-Rhine and Rhône-Rhine canals led to the construction of a new port near Porte de l'Hôpital. Ten years later another port, the Metzgertorhafen, was opened a little further to the east at the level of Porte des Bouchers (Butchers' Gate). In 1918 it was renamed Port du Bassin d'Austerlitz. Finally, between 1899 and 1901 the port was moved to its present site on the banks of the Rhine to the east of the city. And the harbour master's office (see opposite) and the trade and industry basins were built. The channelling of the Rhine begun in 1898 by the German administration imposed this last move, which was completed in 1901.

Strasbourg's autonomous port is the second-largest river port in France (and the fourth in Europe, after Duisburg, Paris and Liège), and the main business park in Alsace.

Extending over 100 km, it comprises Strasbourg's main port and the adjacent ports of Lauterbourg, Beinheim and Marckolsheim (200 hectares) as well as loading stations along the Rhine at Seltz, Fort-Louis, Dalpressa, Drusenheim, Offendorf, Gerstheim and Rhinau.

The Rhine is now the Europe's main inland waterway, and the world's busiest commercial river.

LA FERME BUSSIERRE

(25)

Understanding nature to better protect it

Centre d'initiation à la nature et à l'environnement (CINE) de Strasbourg Eurométropole
155, rue Kempf
03 88 35 89 56
sinestrasbourg.org
Programme and prices of activities available on the website
Children's workshops on Wednesday afternoons

Little known to most Strasbourg residents, La Ferme Bussierre lies between the Château de Pourtalès park and the Robertsau forest – one of the city's most peaceful green spaces. Since 2001, a former barn here has housed the Centre d'Initiation à la Nature et à l'Environnement (CINE), run by the Strasbourg Initiation Nature Environnement association (SINE). To raise visitors' awareness of the fragility of natural heritage, the farm offers a range of activities to discover biodiversity around the city and suburbs in a fun way.

The centre promotes awareness of biodiversity in urban and peri-urban areas through fun, educational activities. CINE organises guided nature walks led by specialists, covering themes like the Canotiers trail, Rhine forest species, insects near local ponds, wild mammals in the city, and the unique 'Rhin Tortu' (or 'Krimmeri') – an unchannelled river system linking the Rhine and the Ill.

In addition to adult workshops, exhibitions, debates and volunteering, CINE offers Wednesday sessions for children. These include composting, papermaking, natural household product creation, gardening, cooking and more.

Many events are repeated yearly, such as the Festival of Bees and Biodiversity, Nature and Heritage Days, Night of the Stars, and International Bat Night. Ahead of Christmas, CINE also runs workshops for baking bredeles, traditional Alsatian biscuits.

The farm itself – sometimes spelled 'Bussière' – was once an outbuilding of the Château de Pourtalès. It was built in 1876 by Alsatian architect Louis-Michel Boltz for Baron Alfred Renouard de Bussière, father of Mélanie de Bussière, the future Countess of Pourtalès.

Outside the centre

Parc de Pourtalès
1
2
3
4
5
6
Wacken
Robertsau
Bassin Albert Auberger
Parlement européen
p. 204
Canal de la Marne au Rhin
Parc de l'Orangerie
Quartier des XV
Jardin botanique
Bassin des Remparts
Bassin du Commerce
Bassin de l'Industrie
Rhin
Allemagne
Pont d'Anvers
p. 92
Parc de la Citadelle
Canal du Rhône au Rhin
Bassin Vauban
28
Kehl
Pont de l'Europe
KARLSRUHE, FREIBURG IM BREISGAU
7
Jardin des Deux Rives
Pont Vauban
Neudorf

FL. B 442 LAUNCH

①

A Second World War launch, still afloat

MM Park France
4, rue Gutenberg
67610 La Wantzenau
03 88 59 25 43
mmpark.fr
contact@mmpark.fr
Timetables on the website

Just minutes from Strasbourg, visitors will find a surprising sight — a Second World War launch docked in a lifelike naval base setting. Poised as if ready to cast off, this boat is one of the standout features of the impressive MM Park France (see following pages).

Built in August 1944, the Flugbetriebsboot Seeteufel ('Sea Devil') Klasse B IV-5 — registration 'Fl. B 442' — measures 20 metres long and 3.6 metres wide, with a weight of around 18 tonnes. It could accommodate eight crew members and reach speeds of 21.5 knots (about 40 km/h). Assigned to the Luftwaffe (German Air Force) stationed in the Netherlands, its mission was to rescue downed pilots from the North Sea.

Neglected after the war, the boat remained docked in Amsterdam with only minimal upkeep. It was eventually acquired by collector Éric Kauffmann and transferred to La Wantzenau. In June 2012, it was entrusted to the Association de Sauvegarde du Patrimoine Historique Militaire (ASPHM).

Following 15 months in dry dock and 4 more after re-floating, the boat was fully restored to its original state: repainted and re-equipped with original features like its duckboard, buoys, lanterns, navigation lights and electrical boxes. Post-war modifications were removed.

Today, Fl. B 442 floats in a specially designed 30-metre-long basin. It's part of a reconstructed naval base scene complete with ammo crates, a naval mine with mooring cable*, and ambient sea sounds played over speakers. Visitors can step aboard and take the helm — forgetting, if only briefly, that the engine no longer works and its two propellers were removed during restoration.

**A mooring cable is a steel rope connecting a mine to a heavy ballast on the seabed.*

MM Park France : the incredible collection of a tank enthusiast

Off the usual tourist trail, MM Park France in La Wantzenau offers a remarkable exhibition dedicated to the Second World War.

Open to the public since 1 March 2017, this private enterprise occupies a former printing house bought by tank enthusiast Éric Kauffmann to showcase his personal collection.

Over 20 years of acquisitions across Europe, Russia and the United States are displayed across no less than 7,000 square metres.

The incredibly rich collection includes more than 120 vehicles (some still in good working order), guns of all sizes, a U-boat turret, an observation bell from the Atlantic Wall, a Luftwaffe speedboat (see previous double-page spread), a fighter plane, over 400 uniforms (including a rare series of women's uniforms), as well as hundreds of assault rifles, pistols, machine guns, mines and other explosives. Kauffmann's collection is managed by the Association de Sauvegarde du Patrimoine Historique Militaire (ASPHM), whose members still restore and maintain the vehicles (on the edge of the site's car park several tanks wait to be refurbished).

One of the attractions of MM Park France is the hands-on, interactive experience sought by this exhibition, which required more than seven years of preparation.

The 'park' is different from most museums by the proximity of the exhibits. With the exception of fragile uniforms, protected by display cases, visitors can touch vehicles, look round them, or even take a seat.

They can handle the controls of an anti-aircraft gun, or climb into a machine gun nest with a genuine (deactivated) MG-42.

There's also a small restaurant, making this a destination for history enthusiasts and families alike.

'Plan Sussex': an operation that greatly contributed to the success of the Allied landing in Normandy

In comparison with the monumental collection of Éric Kauffmann (see opposite), the 400 objects gathered by his friend Dominique Soulier, displayed in a modest room on the first floor of MM Park France, might seem insignificant.

Yet they concern a secret mission codenamed 'Plan Sussex', which was critical to the success of the Allied landings in Normandy. This mission, little known even among historians of the Second World War, was planned in March 1943 by General Eisenhower's staff. It involved parachuting plain clothes officers working in pairs (observer and radio operator) into several strategic locations in occupied France.

Their task was to inform the Allies of the number and position of German troops, especially Panzer divisions. A total of 120 French volunteers were extensively trained in military intelligence techniques (military espionage, radio operation and covert survival) by the British and American services. The 'Sussex' collection includes the spies' false ID papers, miniature radios and cameras, and weapons disguised as everyday objects – a rare tribute to the bravery of these unsung heroes.

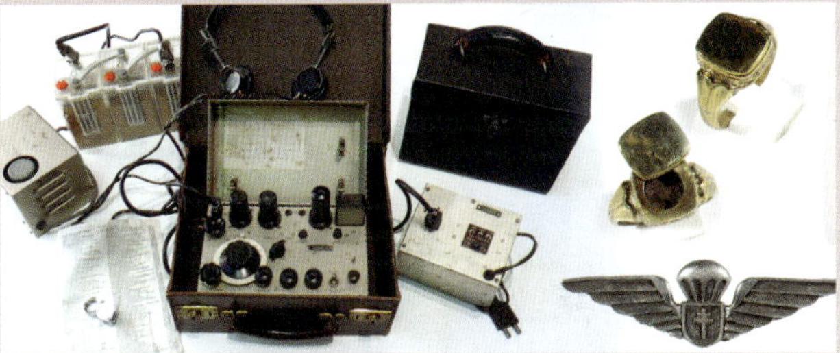

'LE GÉNIE DU LIEU' SCULPTURE

②

An artistic illusion

Parc de Pourtalès
161, rue Mélanie
Bus C1, C15 – Robertsau Lamproie stop then about 20 min walk

'Le Génie du Lieu' ('Spirit of the Place'), by Italian artist Giulio Paolini, is an intriguing sculpture that plays with our perceptions and sense of place. Created in 2001 especially for Pourtalès Park, the work depicts a crouching figure pointing a finger at a detailed map of the park at his feet, seemingly guiding the visitor.

At first glance, 'Le Génie du Lieu' destabilises with its illusions. Although the figure appears to be realistically cast in bronze, it is in fact made of synthetic resin and fibreglass. Similarly, the map beneath it, supposedly meant to guide, is deliberately misleading: the compass rose is incorrect, and the labels do not always correspond to the sculptures in the park.

Paolini plays with representation and reality, reminding us that any attempt to freeze a place on a map is always an imperfect abstraction. The work consists of four parts: the first map under the character's feet, a second smaller map with seven small spheres indicating other sculptures in the park, a third element that gathers natural debris from the park (earth, leaves, insects), and a fourth that decomposes and merges with the undergrowth. This progressive process symbolises both the fading of representation and the return of art to nature. The greenish patina of the sculpture accentuates this effect of ageing and disappearance.

With its classical posture and proportions, 'Le Génie du Lieu' is striking for its contemporary approach. The installation has no pedestal, standing at the same level as visitors, breaking with monumental tradition. The modern suit, complete with tie and jacket, further connects the sculpture to our time.

In fact, the sculpture is something of an artistic joke: an illusion of noble material, an illusion of accurate orientation, an illusion of faithful representation of the park. Anyone seeking to interpret it is left uncertain and disoriented. In the end, you must get lost to fully understand the work and its surroundings.

'DÉTOUR' SCULPTURE

③

A discreet yet effective work

Parc de Pourtalès - 161, rue Mélanie
Bus C1, C15 – Robertsau Lamproie stop then about 20 min walk

The spectacular 'Détour' sculpture (2005) by Jimmie Durham, in Strasbourg's Parc de Pourtalès, often goes unnoticed. Yet this fascinating artwork questions our relationship with nature and human intervention. Durham, an American artist of Cherokee origin, is known for his critical take on society and culture. His militant yet poetic work balances humour with protest.

'Détour' consists of an imposing block of rough granite, extracted from a local quarry. This massive, oval-shaped stone evokes millennia of slow, irresistible natural processes. Wrapping awkwardly around it is an orange pipe, the kind typically used in urban infrastructure. Instead of following a natural curve, the pipe forms an angular, rigid path over the stone. It seems to simultaneously enclose the rock and yield to its presence – like

a snake emerging from the ground before diving back underground. The contrast highlights the tension between nature and human intervention. The pipe, with its absurd right angles, symbolises the desire to control and regulate the environment. The stone, by contrast, represents resistance to such constraints. This opposition is common in art, but Durham tackles it here in a direct, confrontational way.

The piece also echoes Native American traditions. The curved shape of the pipe recalls the tumulus of the Great Serpent Mound, an ancient Native American earthwork in Ohio (USA), where culture and nature intertwine.

Encased by this intrusive structure, the granite boulder becomes a symbol of struggle and resilience, like the Cherokee tomahawk.

Beyond its reflection on the clash between nature and culture, 'Détour' also criticises consumer society. It highlights human excess and reminds us of the humility we should have in the face of natural forces. This message echoes in other works by Durham – notably his famous performance in which he stones a refrigerator, mocking our attachment to material possessions.

'LA FORÊT REGARDE ET ÉCOUTE' ④ ARTWORK

A meeting between nature and humanity

Parc de Pourtalès
161, rue Mélanie
Bus C1, C15 – Robertsau Lamproie stop then about 20 min walk

'La Forêt Regarde et Écoute' (1999–2004, 'The Forest Looks and Listens') in Parc de Pourtalès is a discreet yet fascinating work by Italian artist Claudio Parmiggiani (b. 1943).

Little known and often overlooked, the artwork was originally composed of 14 bronze ears attached to beech trees, each measuring around 1.10 metres – proportional to the size of the trees. After the 1999 storm, only seven of these ears remained.

The installation also involved cutting certain branches to create eye-shaped scars on the beeches. Together, the bronze ears and the eye-like marks symbolically transform the forest into a conscious space of observation and listening.

Associated with the *Arte Povera* (Poor Art) movement, Parmiggiani plays here with the ambiguity of perception: while we observe nature, it observes us in return.

This inverted dialogue gives the work a spiritual and philosophical depth, reminiscent of Druidic worship sites or Zen gardens, where the deliberate positioning of elements prevents any single, complete perspective.

The piece also speaks to learning and the transmission of knowledge. Ears and eyes serve as vectors of understanding, emphasising the role of nature in the development of civilisations. It suggests a necessary symbiosis between humanity and the environment – a foundational communion essential to survival.

Finally, the work carries symbolic weight: in certain cultures, the ear is associated with fertility, while in Italian tradition, the tree trunk evokes the male (*yang*) principle.

The installation thus becomes an allegory of creation, representing the balance between humanity and nature.

Arte povera

An Italian art movement originating in Turin and Rome, *Arte Povera* emerged on the international art scene in the 1960s. The term *povera* (poor) reflects its emphasis on simplicity and its opposition to the extravagance of consumerist production.

‘LES ARBRORIGÈNES’ ARTWORK ⑤

Human-tree symbiosis

Parc de Pourtalès
161, rue Mélanie
Bus C1, C15 – Robertsau Lamproie stop then about 20 min walk

'Les Arbrorigènes' (1988; 'Arbrogenes') by Ernest Pignon-Ernest is an extraordinary artwork in Parc de Pourtalès. Originally composed of ten male and female figures, moulded in silicone and reproduced in polyurethane foam, only five remain today following the 1999 storm. These sculptures depict human forms climbing trees and merging with the bark.

Their plant-like skin mimics the surrounding colours, making them almost invisible. Blending into the landscape – often hidden by foliage – they form a particularly discreet and almost secretive work.

Pignon-Ernest (b. 1942, Nice) lives and works in Paris. A pioneer of street art, he is best known for pasting images of human figures into urban spaces. His committed and politically engaged art explores the memory of places and the relationship between people and their environment.

His work often draws on mythology and literature, such as Ovid's 'Metamorphoses', in which people are transformed into trees. Here, however, he adds a scientific dimension. With help from biologist Claude Gudin, the sculptures were infused with life: a billion micro-algae embedded in the surface allowed them to photosynthesise. During the day, they absorbed carbon dioxide and released oxygen; at night, they breathed like us.

Beyond this biological experimentation, 'Les Arbrorigènes' raises deeper questions about humanity's original connection to nature. Half human, half plant, the figures symbolise our dependence on ecosystems and the fragile balance between civilisation and the natural world.

'LEUR LIEU' INSTALLATION

6

A secret magical world for 137 bronze elves

Parc de Pourtalès
161, rue Mélanie
Bus C1, C15 – Robertsau Lamproie stop then about 20 min walk

© Bonio

'Leur Lieu' (1995; 'Their Place') by Jean-Marie Krauth is a surprising installation of 137 bronze elves, often overlooked, scattered around a grove in Parc de Pourtalès.

These little elves, all cast from the same mould, have no hands, faces or tools. Unlike traditional garden gnomes, their anonymity and stillness are unsettling. Randomly distributed through the undergrowth, they appear to be part of the landscape, evoking the impression of a hidden, parallel world.

The title 'Leur Lieu' carries a double meaning: both a microcosm for these mysterious beings and a macrocosm for the visitor. What the work lacks in monumentality, it makes up for in numbers: spotting just one elf suggests an entire unseen population.

Krauth draws inspiration from Rhenish legends, according to which elves – always wearing a cap – are born from acorns that fall on magical ground. Here, the grove becomes their cradle, a sanctuary where they seem to rise from the earth. The artist also subverts the traditional moulding technique used to create chocolate figurines of St Nicholas: by employing two halves of a mould, he freezes his elves in classical sculptural poses.

Through this installation, Krauth questions the very nature of sculpture. Where classical works impose fixity, 'Leur Lieu' suggests latent movement – as if the elves might disappear the moment we look away.

By blending scholarly culture with popular folklore, Krauth invites visitors to rediscover the park with fresh, poetic eyes.

Born in 1944 in Haguenau, Krauth lives and works in Strasbourg. As a sculptor and installation artist, he explores a variety of materials – including lead, iron, glass and brick – combining artistic creation with the memory of places. His work challenges notions of reality through the lens of fantasy.

'IZANAÏA' AND 'OTO-DATE-STEPS' INSTALLATIONS ⑦

Invitation to the sound ceremony

Jardin des Deux Rives
Bus 2 – Cirque stop – Centre Équestre stop

In the heart of the Jardin des Deux Rives, a cross-border space between Strasbourg and Kehl, Japanese artist Akio Suzuki has discreetly installed two remarkable works: 'Izanaïa' (2004) and 'Oto-date-steps'. Invisible to those who don't know how to look, they transform a simple stroll into a sanctuary of listening.

The word *Izanaïa* comes from the Japanese verb *izanau*, meaning 'invite' or 'guide'. The work takes the form of two curved walls of pink sandstone, built in dry masonry from Vosges stone, like the *bories* (shepherd's huts) of the Luberon. This choice is significant: sandstone, a local material both porous and dense, is used here as an acoustic instrument. The stones are stacked without mortar, allowing sound to vibrate between them. The two walls form a sinuous corridor, their parabolic shape channelling sounds and directing them towards a precise central point.

Complementary and more discreet, 'Oto-date-steps' (from *oto*, meaning 'sound', and *nodate*, meaning 'open-air tea ceremony') consists of engraved plates bearing patterns in the form of ears and footsteps that invite visitors to stop and try to perceive the invisible. As you approach the centre, the sounds of the environment – the wall of water, the Rhine, birdsong, the rustling of the wind – grow in intensity, and where the walls come closer together, listening is amplified and takes on greater significance.

At this junction, Suzuki suggests that two people can stand back-to-back, sharing a silent moment of listening, an intimacy without words. The work then becomes a sensory bridge, a form of primitive communication – profound, and freed from language.

These tiles were not laid at random. Their placement was chosen according to the site's acoustic characteristics: echo zones, resonance points between the Rhine and the wall of water. The passer-by, invited to walk 'by ear', enters into a kind of sound ceremony akin to the tea ceremony: slow, refined, attentive.

Both works are part of a profound artistic process – making listening a conscious, almost sacred act. Listening here becomes a symbol of dialogue: between France and Germany, between human beings and nature, between the visible and the invisible.

Where words may fail, sound flows freely.

OULIPO'S 'TROLL DE TRAM' ⑧

A literary artwork waiting for the tram

On top of Wilmotte columns along Line A

In 1994, the Strasbourg members of the OuLiPo group (see opposite) took over the city with 'Troll de Tram', a literary creation both original and little known, installed on the iconic Wilmotte advertising columns. The work reflects a desire to integrate literature into the daily lives of Strasbourgeois in a discreet yet imaginative way. Comprising 96 texts displayed on the columns at Line A stations, it offers travellers a playful and poetic experience. 'Troll de Tram' plays with station names, sounds and narrative structures to transform an ordinary journey into a literary adventure. The pieces take several different forms, each exploring a specific constraint.

The 'Notices toponymiques' ('Toponymic Notes'), written in the style of dictionary entries, invent fanciful etymologies for each station name. For Étoile station, the entry reads : *ÉTOILE, marque déposée. La société fabricante de Sels d'Alsace est restée célèbre pour son slogan vantant l'efficacité de son sel de Potasse : 'Étoile déneige'* ('STAR, registered trademark. The manufacturer of Sels d'Alsace has remained famous for its slogan praising the effectiveness of its potash salt: Étoile déneige [lit. 'Snow cleared from star']').

The *Récit au beau présent* is like a soap opera developing the plot station by station, following a strict rule: each episode can only use the letters of that station's name.

Langage cuit hijacks famous expressions and titles by adding 'tram' or 'tramway': *La nuit, tous les trams sont gris / Autant en emporte le tram* (At night, all trams are grey [a play on the film title 'La nuit, tous les chats sont gris' / 'At Night, All Cats Are Grey'] / 'Gone with the tram' ['Autant en emporte le vent', French title of 'Gone with the Wind']).

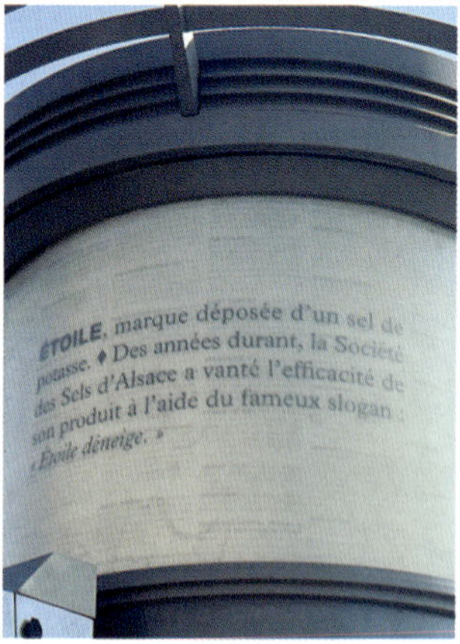

As for *Variations homophoniques*, they play on sound, such as *Le tramway de Strasbourg* becoming *Les trois muets de cédrat se bourrent* (lit. 'The three mutes of citrus get stoned').

In December 2023, some of these signs disappeared during urban renovations.

What is OuLiPo?

Ouvroir de Littérature Potentielle, better known as OuLiPo, is a literary research group founded in 1960 by writer Raymond Queneau and mathematician François Le Lionnais, with the aim of discovering new potentials for language and modernising expression through writing games. OuLiPo is also defined by what it is not: 'It is not a literary movement; it is not a scientific seminar; it is not random literature; its research is naive, artisanal and fun.'

The group is famous for mathematical challenges imposed on language, requiring creative tricks, based on the belief that constraint provokes originality and encourages the search for inventive solutions. One of its best-known techniques is the lipogram, a composition systematically omitting a particular letter (as in Georges Perec's novel 'La Disparition', written entirely without the letter 'e'); or S+7, which replaces each noun in a text with the seventh word that follows it in the dictionary. Raymond Queneau famously transformed La Fontaine's fable 'La Cigale et la Fourmi' ('The Grasshopper and the Ant') into 'La Cimaise et la Fraction' ('The Picture Rail and the Fraction'). Other playful forms include snowballs – poems in which each line grows by one letter – and the *Contrainte du prisonnier (Prisoner's Constraint)*, in which a prisoner with limited paper avoids letters with ascenders or descenders, such as b, d, f, g, h, i, j, k, l, p, q, t, y. OuLiPo even has its own calendar: 'An Oulipian year, given the intellectual energy it requires, is worth at least a century of the normal calendar.'

Among the most famous works published by Oulipians are 'Cent mille milliards de poèmes' by Raymond Queneau, 'La Vie mode d'emploi' ('Life: A User's Manual') by Georges Perec, and 'Si par une nuit d'hiver un voyageur' ('If on a Winter's Night a Traveller') by Italo Calvino.

Membership in OuLiPo is by invitation only, provided that the invited member has never asked to join. Election must be unanimous, and any invitee is free to refuse (refusal is final). Once accepted, members can only resign 'by committing suicide in front of the bailiff'. Even after death, members remain Oulipians, simply 'excused for reason of death'.

No fixed definition has ever been given for the concept of 'potentiality', which lies at the heart of OuLiPo's name. As member Daniel Levin Becker explains: 'This is to everyone's advantage. When you don't know what you're looking for, your chances of finding it increase. This remains an ideal that each member is free to pursue in their own way.'

COLONNE NAPOLÉON

⑨

A little-known testimony to the Imperial desire to organise territory

Route du Rhin
Corner of Cimetière Saint-Urbain
Tram D, E – Star-Polygone stop

In Strasbourg, along the Route du Rhin, the Napoléon Column is a discreet monument that often goes unnoticed.

Yet it is one of the few remaining visible traces of the vast road redevelopment programme launched by Prefect Adrien Lezay-Marnésia between 1810 and 1814.

By that time, the Napoleonic wars had severely damaged the transport infrastructure.

To improve traffic and guide travellers, marker columns were erected at all the main crossroads. Ten such columns remain in Alsace today. Like the one in Illkirch, at the Colonne tram stop, Strasbourg's column is a little-known reminder of this Imperial ambition to impose order on the landscape.

Made of sandstone, the Napoléon Column is distinguished by its elegance, its moulded pedestal, and its Ionic marble shaft. On top sits a pink sandstone globe, itself crowned with a small bronze cross – a distinctive feature of road markers from that era.

Two oval inscriptions engraved on the shaft indicate precise distances:
– East: Kehl, 4 km
– South: Illkirch-Graffenstaden, 6.36 km

Until 1870, this column stood at the exit of Strasbourg, at the Porte d'Austerlitz, where travellers faced a choice: to take the road east towards Germany and Vienna, or continue south towards Colmar and Lyon.

During major renovation work on Place de l'Étoile in the 1980s, the monument was moved to its current location by the Saint-Urbain cemetery.

It may barely catch the eye of passers-by today, but the Napoléon Column remains a valuable historical relic, recalling a key moment in Strasbourg's urban history.

More than a decorative feature, it symbolises Napoleon Bonaparte's determination to bring order to the territory and clarity to the road network.

ART NOUVEAU BUILDING AT 55, ROUTE DU POLYGONE

⑩

The full-size business card of a local architect

55, route du Polygone
67100 Neudorf

© Aline Haucq

The Neudorf district was a favourite source of inspiration for Aloys Walther, an architect born in Rosheim in 1869 who died in Strasbourg in 1926.

In 1904 he designed the striking building at 55 route du Polygone. Combining apartments with a ground-floor business, it is richly decorated across the façade.

Walther also established his architectural practice there, making the building his business card.

The frontage is dominated by a vast oriel window extending over several floors.

On either side are balconies, with Art Nouveau iron railings flowing from one to the next, culminating at the top in a flower that seems to turn with the sun. The balustrade pattern evokes sunbeams and the wings of birds.

The most spectacular element is the ceramic fan-shaped panel crowning the building, decorated with a sunset, flowers and birds.

Flanking the oriel are ten smaller ceramic panels depicting blue and green dragonflies set against a sun partly veiled by clouds.

Other works by Walther in the neighbourhood include

– 79, 98a, 166, rue du Polygone
– 4 and 5, rue Jules Rathgeber
– 19, rue d'Erstein

RELIEF OF A BEE CARVED IN A HEXAGRAM

(11)

The traditional symbol of breweries

97, avenue de Colmar
Tram A – Schlutfeld stop

At the intersection of Avenue de Colmar and Rue de Mulhouse stands a building from the turn of the 20th century, designed by architect Aloys Walter. Above the second-floor windows of the corner oriel is a little-known sculpted relief.

At its centre, a stone bee rests on a six-pointed star (a hexagram, also known as the Seal of Solomon). The star is framed by ears of wheat, vine leaves, and bunches of grapes. On either side of the bee appear the dates 1896 and 1902, corresponding to the period of the building's construction.

Commissioned by G. Roser, the building originally housed a café-brasserie on the ground floor, which explains the relief. The hexagram, or star of the brewers, was traditionally used in Alsace as a sign for breweries (see opposite).

The bee, with its six legs, six abdominal segments, and hexagonal cells, reinforces this symbolism while also evoking the collective effort of beer making.

The ears of wheat recall the raw material essential for brewing, while the grapes and vine leaves remind us that wine too was served in such establishments.

What is the brewers' star?

The brewers' star (also known as the brewer's cross) is an ancient symbol whose use has been documented since 1397 in the brewing community.

It is identical to the six-pointed star also known as the hexagram (or Seal of Solomon, see p. 63), formed by the intertwining of two equilateral triangles (one pointing upwards and the other downwards) which symbolize the spiritual and human nature of Man, i.e., the union of Man with his creator.

Also presented since ancient times (well before the beginning of Christianity) as a talisman to enjoy God's blessing and offer protection against evil spirits, the hexagram only became a Jewish symbol in the Middle Ages.

At a time when, due to a lack of scientific knowledge, the success of brewing was as uncertain as it was mysterious, and brewers attributed their failures to invisible forces, the star served as a protective talisman, warding off evil spirits, preventing fires and guaranteeing the purity of the beverage.

It also symbolically represents the alchemy of brewing, which brings together the four elements (earth, fire, water and air): earth provides the grain, water and air enable germination, water and fire produce the brew, and fire and air trigger fermentation.

In alchemy, these four elements are each represented by an equilateral triangle that forms a hexagram.

Over time, the brewers' star was also used on signs to indicate the presence of a brewery, particularly in the Rhineland and Bavaria. It can also be found on containers containing beer. Its use declined from the 18th century onwards.

SCHULMEISTER OBELISK

⑫

Curious Masonic and Egyptian symbols

1, route de la Meinau (corner of Avenue de Colmar)
Tram A – Émile Mathis stop

At the corner of Avenue de Colmar stands a discreet obelisk, often overlooked by passers-by. Erected in 1806 by Friedrich Weinbrenner, it once marked the entrance to the sumptuous estate

of Charles-Louis Schulmeister (1770–1853), Napoleon Bonaparte's favourite spy (see following double-page spread).

This 4-metre-high column, carved from Jaumont stone (sourced from quarries near Metz), was originally designed to point the way towards Schulmeister's château (now lost) and its surrounding grounds (see below). Intended as a luxurious neoclassical residence, the estate was even conceived as a potential stopover for Napoleon himself.

What sets this obelisk apart is its allegorical decoration, inspired by the Egyptian and Masonic motifs that were fashionable during the Consulate and the Empire. Among its many engravings is the ouroboros – a serpent biting its own tail, symbolising reincarnation and divine enlightenment.

This motif is positioned at the very top of the obelisk. One side features a seated pharaoh, depicted at a perfect right angle – a symbol of equity – holding an equilateral triangle representing the ternary system, the foundation of Masonic doctrine. On another face of the obelisk, a carved figure may depict Anubis, the Egyptian god of embalming and master of necropolises.

A spy likely behind the name of Meinau district

The inscription *Strasse nach Meinau* ('Road to Meinau') carved into the obelisk recalls how, in 1806 – the same year Schulmeister acquired the vast estate at Entenfang (Duck Decoy) – he renamed it Meine Aue ('My Meadows').

Charles Louis Schulmeister (1770–1853): extraordinary life of Napoleon Bonaparte's favourite spy

Born in 1770 in Baden (north of Freiburg), not far from Strasbourg, Charles Louis Schulmeister had already amassed a fortune from smuggling by 1800. His sharp business sense and skill at concealing information soon caught the attention of the future emperor. After a meeting in Paris in 1804, arranged by the future General Rapp, Napoleon made Schulmeister one of his trusted spies. Clever, cunning and fiercely devoted to Napoleon, Schulmeister quickly became one of the most skilled and discreet double agents of the Imperial police. He was gradually entrusted with increasingly secret missions, earning a reputation as a brilliant intelligence master in the emperor's service. At the start of the 1805 Ulm Campaign (part of the War of the Third Coalition), Schulmeister entered the besieged city of Ulm in disguise. Posing as a Hungarian, he repeatedly met with Austrian General Karl Mack. These encounters are thought to have contributed to Mack's puzzling decision to surrender after the Battle of Ulm: Schulmeister allegedly led Mack to believe that a coup d'état was underway to overthrow Napoleon. He even went as far as forging a fake newspaper to convince him. As a result, Mack stayed in Ulm, awaiting allies who never came – sealing his defeat. Schulmeister's daring was such that he even took part in a council of war in the presence of the Austrian emperor, after bribing an Austrian general for access. Following the capture of Vienna, Napoleon appointed him Commissioner General of the city's police from 15 November 1805 to mid-January 1806. Schulmeister maintained order throughout the occupation with only a modest force. His exploits didn't end there. During the Prussian Campaign, on the night of 4 November 1806, Schulmeister captured the city of Wismar with just seven men, taking about 15 officers and 100 soldiers prisoner. From Wismar, he went on to seize Rostock with 25 hussars, where he found 18 ships anchored in the harbour. Cunning and charismatic, Schulmeister's mastery of manipulation rather than brute strength soon made him a legend among intelligence agents. But the fall of the Empire brought his career and fortune to an end. In 1833, ruined, he was forced to sell his estate. He is buried in Saint-Urbain cemetery in Strasbourg, never having received the Legion of Honour he so desired – a decoration Napoleon, curiously, never awarded him.

AU NID DE CIGOGNES RESTAURANT

⑬

Former administrative building of the 1895 Exhibition

102, route de Schirmeck

Few people travelling along Route de Schirmeck realise that Au Nid de Cigognes (At the Storks' Nest) restaurant occupies one of Strasbourg's important historical buildings.

During the Industrial and Craft Exhibition of Alsace-Lorraine, Baden and the Palatinate, held at Parc de l'Orangerie from May to October 1895 (see p. 240), architect Ludwig Bettcher designed an administrative building in regional style. This blend of half-timbering and ashlar stone was named *Storchennest* – literally 'stork's nest'.

At the close of the exhibition, the building was dismantled, transported, and reassembled stone by stone on its present site. It is one of only two surviving structures from the exhibition, the other being the Buerehiesel restaurant (see p. 238).

Faithful to the *fin de siècle* spirit – a cultural and ideological movement that sought to preserve landscapes, housing, local customs and traditions against the upheavals of industrialisation and urbanisation – the façade reflects the sober lines and frameworks of peasant houses, while also showcasing traditional decorative motifs.

Although the building does not fall within the UNESCO World Heritage site (Strasbourg, Grande-Île and Neustadt), it is still carefully maintained under the local urban plan, which ensures the preservation of regional authenticity.

It was September 1995 and Thomas Jonglez was in Peshawar, the northern Pakistani city 20 kilometres from the tribal zone he was to visit a few days later. It occurred to him that he should record the hidden aspects of his native city, Paris, which he knew so well. During his seven-month trip back home from Beijing, the countries he crossed took in Tibet (entering clandestinely, hidden under blankets in an overnight bus), Iran and Kurdistan. He never took a plane but travelled by boat, train or bus, hitchhiking, cycling, on horseback or on foot, reaching Paris just in time to celebrate Christmas with the family.

On his return, he spent two fantastic years wandering the streets of the capital to gather material for his first 'secret guide', written with a friend. For the next seven years he worked in the steel industry until the passion for discovery overtook him. He launched Jonglez Publishing in 2003 and moved to Venice three years later.

In 2013, in search of new adventures, the family left Venice and spent six months travelling to Brazil, via North Korea, Micronesia, the Solomon Islands, Easter Island, Peru and Bolivia.

After seven years in Rio de Janeiro, he now lives in Berlin with his wife and three children.

Jonglez Publishing produces a range of titles in nine languages, released in 40 countries.

ATLASES

Atlas of abandoned France
Atlas of extreme weather
Atlas of forbidden places
Atlas of geographical curiosities
Atlas of geographical curiosities – Britain
Atlas of unusual wines

PHOTO BOOKS

Abandoned America
Abandoned Asylums
Abandoned Australia
Abandoned Belgium
Abandoned Churches: Unclaimed places of worship
Abandoned cinemas of the world
Abandoned France
Abandoned Germany
Abandoned Italy
Abandoned Japan
Abandoned Lebanon
Abandoned Spain
Abandoned USSR
Abandoned world – An AI-generated exploration
After the Final Curtain – The Fall of the American Movie Theater
After the Final Curtain – America's Abandoned Theaters
Baikonur – Vestiges of the Soviet space programme
Cinemas – A French heritage
Clickbait – A visual journey through AIgenerated stories
Forbidden France
Forbidden Places – Vol. 1
Forbidden Places – Vol. 2
Forbidden Places – Vol. 3
Forgotten France
Forgotten Heritage
Oblivion
Secret sacred sites
Venice deserted
Venice from the skies

'SOUL OF' GUIDES

Soul of Amsterdam
Soul of Athens
Soul of Barcelona
Soul of Berlin
Soul of Brussels
Soul of Detroit
Soul of Kyoto
Soul of Lisbon
Soul of Los Angeles
Soul of Marrakesh
Soul of Marseille
Soul of Milan
Soul of New York
Soul of Paris
Soul of Rome
Soul of Tokyo
Soul of Venice
Soul of Vienna

SECRET ATLASES

London – The secret atlas
New York – The secret atlas
Paris – The secret atlas
Venice – The secret atlas

'SECRET' GUIDES

Secret Amsterdam
Secret Bali – An unusual guide
Secret Bangkok
Secret Barcelona
Secret Bath – An unusual guide
Secret Belfast
Secret Berlin
Secret Boston – An unusual guide
Secret Brighton – An unusual guide
Secret Brooklyn – An unusual guide
Secret Brussels
Secret Budapest
Secret Buenos Aires
Secret Campania
Secret Cape Town
Secret Copenhagen
Secret Dolomites
Secret Dublin – An unusual guide
Secret Edinburgh – An unusual guide
Secret Florence
Secret French Riviera
Secret Geneva
Secret Glasgow – An unusual guide
Secret Granada
Secret Helsinki
Secret Istanbul
Secret Johannesburg
Secret Lisbon
Secret Liverpool – An unusual guide
Secret London – An unusual guide
Secret London – Unusual bars & restaurants
Secret Los Angeles – An unusual guide
Secret Louisiana – An unusual guide
Secret Madrid
Secret Mexico City
Secret Milan
Secret Montreal – An unusual guide
Secret Naples
Secret New Orleans – An unusual guide
Secret New York – An unusual guide
Secret New York – Curious activities
Secret New York – Hidden bars & restaurants
Secret Normandy
Secret Paris
Secret Potsdam
Secret Prague
Secret Provence
Secret Rio de Janeiro
Secret Rome
Secret Seville
Secret Singapore
Secret Sussex – An unusual guide
Secret Tokyo
Secret Tuscany
Secret Venice
Secret York – An unusual guide

PHOTO CREDITS

All texts and photos are by **Guillaume Bouvier**, **Véronique Herbreteau** and **Isabelle Kaap**, with the exception of:

ClaudeTruong-Ngoc (photos): Medallions on the Quai Kléber (left page)

Roland Burckel (photos): Strasbourg in the Middle Ages: streets littered with rubbish, A potter's emblem, The rooster on Rue de la Nuée Bleue (right page), Animal pavilion frieze, 'La Racine' sculpture (right page), Colonne Napoléon, Schulmeister obelisk (left page)

Jocelyne Boes (photo): Vestiges of a fountain (left page)

Archives de la ville et de l'Eurométropole (Bibliothèque) (photo): Vestiges of a fountain (right page)

PortableNYCTours (photo): 'Le Son' et 'La Lumière' bas-reliefs (right page)

S R. (photos): Reliefs at 12–14, rue du 22 Novembre (right page)

Letazwiki: Symbolism of the triquetra (triskelion) (top photo)

Alain Van den Hende: Symbolism of the triquetra (triskelion) (bottom photo)

Ralph Hammann (photos): Veronica's veil at Saint-Pierre-le-Vieux, Cloister of Saint-Pierre-le-Jeune protestant church, Sculpture of a lansquenet on Rue des Hallebardes

Tangopaso (photo): Sculpture of a lansquenet with a dog

Frédéric Lix (photo): Lohkäs' sign (right page)

Franzfoto (photo): Origin of the pretzel

Tilman2007 (photo): Relief with three hares

Cendrars83 (photo): Frescoes on the first floor of the former Pharmacie du Cerf (left page)

Yves Trotzier (photo): Bibliothèque Pythagore

Bibliothèque Pythagore de Strasbourg (photo): Marthe North-Sigried

Philippoteaux (photo): The affair of the Queen's Necklace: the role of the city of Strasbourg (left page)

Château de Breteuilsha (photo): The affair of the Queen's Necklace: the role of the city of Strasbourg (right page)

Ji-Elle (photo): The rooster on Rue de la Nuée Bleue (left page)

JLPC (photos): The symbolism of the pentragram, the five-pointed star (bottom left page)

Stefanrevollo (photo): Green man from the building at 1, rue Sellénick (left page)

Michel Mus (photo): Green man from the building at 1, rue Sellénick (right page)

Johannes Otto Först (photo): The green man (right page)

Wilfred Helmlinger (photo): Sculpture of the Alsatian (left page), Schulmeister obelisk (right page), Au Nid de Cigognes restaurant (left page)

Studio of Thomas Heinrich Voigt (photo): Effigies of emperor Wilhelm II (right page)

Phil Lewis (photos): Leaktel building façade, Villa Knopf gateway, Cromer building façade (left page and double page)

Fabien Romary (photos): Bueherehiesel restaurant building (left page)

Patrick (photo): Villa Schützenberger façade

BNU (photo): Strasbourg Port du Rhin Post Office: the former harbour master's office at the Port du Rhin

Bonio (photo): 'Leur Lieu' installation (left page)

Aline Haucq (text and photos): Art Nouveau building at 55, route du Polygone

Kaëla Jouini (texts): Veronica's veil at Saint-Pierre-le-Vieux, Bueherehiesel restaurant building, Art Nouveau in Strasbourg, Exposition Industrielle et Artisanale of 1895 in Strasbourg, Building at 14, rue du Général Gouraud, Cromer building façade, Green man from the building at 1, rue Sellénick, Leaktel building façade, Villa Schützenberger façade, Hôtel Brion façade, St Attala's hand, Villa Knopf gateway, Au Nid de Cigognes restaurant

Cartography: **Cyrille Suss** – Layout: **Emmanuelle Willard Toulemonde** –
Translation: **Juliet Powys and Sonny Alexander** – Copy-Editing: **Dikshit Akbari** –
Proofreading: **Abigail Kafka** – Publishing: **Clémence Mathé**

Registration of copyright: October 2025 – Edition: 01
ISBN: 978-2-36195-623-3
Printed in Bulgaria by Dedrax